Praise for *Live Like a Fruit Fly*

"In *Live Like a Fruit Fly,* Gabe Berman shares his recipe for living a more joyful, worthwhile, and abundant life in every way. A witty, entertaining, and insightful read."

—Deepak Chopra
Author, *The Seven Spiritual Laws of Success*

"Meet the new generation of consciousness-raising. Gabe's simple yet profound message can be a life-changer."

—Alan Colmes
Nationally Syndicated Radio Host

"*Live Like a Fruit Fly* is a charming and illuminating book that provides essential wisdom for all of life's complexities. Gabe Berman uses his trademark wit to deliver a blunt and insightful message—live for today, because you cannot count on tomorrow. At times poignant and sobering, *Live Like a Fruit Fly* will leave you thoroughly entertained and enlightened."

—Dr. Sean Kenniff
Author, *Être the Cow* and *Stop Effing Yourself*

LIVE LIKE A FRUIT FLY

The Secret You Already Know

Gabe Berman

Health Communications, Inc.
Deerfield Beach, Florida

www.hcibooks.com

Library of Congress Cataloging-in-Publication Data

Berman, Gabe.
  Live like a fruit fly : the secret you already know / Gabe Berman.
     p. cm.
  ISBN-13: 978-0-7573-1569-5 (trade paper)
  ISBN-10: 0-7573-1569-0 (trade paper)
  ISBN-13: 978-0-7573-9172-9 (e-book)
  ISBN-10: 0-7573-9172-9 (e-book)
  1. Life skills.   2. Conduct of life.   I. Title.
  HQ2037.B467 2011
  646'.7—dc22

                                                   2011012155

Publisher: Health Communications, Inc.
          3201 S.W. 15th Street
          Deerfield Beach, FL 33442–8190

Cover design by Larissa Hise Henoch
Interior design and formatting by Lawna Patterson Oldfield

To the one who never doubted me: *me*

"At night when I go to bed, I ask myself,
'If I don't wake up tomorrow, would I be
proud of how I lived today?'"

—Muhammad Ali, *The Soul of a Butterfly:*
Reflections on Life's Journey

Why Live Like a Fruit Fly?

The average life expectancy of an ordinary fruit fly is in the neighborhood of only a few weeks.

As far as I can tell, fruit flies usually don't sit around watching TV. Fruit flies probably don't waste much time on the Internet. Fruit flies rarely worry about their cell-phone minutes. Fruit flies blink out of existence too quickly to go out of their way to be unkind to other fruit flies.

A fruit fly is born and then buzzes around a bit. It attends to its fruit fly agenda and subsequently succumbs to old age before witnessing a single change of season.

This book is about finding peace and happiness although it might not be immediately apparent from the following sentence:

**You're dying. You've been dying since
the moment you were born.**

Wait.

Stop thinking about what might be on the next page.
Stop thinking about what you might like for dinner.

Wrap your mind around this for a moment: As you read
these words, you're moving closer to the inevitable end.
We all are.

I know you're not an idiot. I know on some level you're
well aware of your own mortality. But if you're anything
like me, you rarely take it into consideration as your
days, months, and years just slip away.

Slip away . . .

Life is short for fruit flies and for us as well. You may
have your whole life ahead of you, but as you grow
older, it seems as though less and less time elapses
between birthdays. If you haven't felt this yet, you will.

I was just four years old. It was early in the morning. The
sun wasn't even shining through the windows yet. I was
wearing a little bathrobe and only had one sock on. I
looked pretty cute.

I opened the fridge and fed Chuckles a piece of Mun-
ster cheese. Chuckles was my black lab. We had to put
him to sleep when I was in the fifth grade.

I blinked and opened my eyes at my high school graduation.

I blinked again and woke up on my thirtieth birthday with fresh wounds from Corporate America. I'm thirty-seven now. Tomorrow I could be sixty.

Unfortunately for some, aging won't be an option. The best-laid plans of mice and men often get severely screwed up. Life is unpredictable. Tsunamis, swine flu, earthquakes, terrorists, magic bullets, spoiled milk . . . you can get hit at any time, from any conceivable angle.

Seize the day.

What does it mean to live like a fruit fly? The hell if I know. I'm joking of course. I just wanted to lighten the mood a bit. But now it's time to *enlighten* the mood.

Does living like a fruit fly mean you should take whatever money you have and blow it on chocolate because you'll be dead by the end of the week anyway?

No.

Does it mean you should jump out of a plane from 15,000 feet with a hastily packed parachute?

Please don't. Statistics show you'll make it to see many more tomorrows.

But you might not. And people who live like fruit flies are well aware of this. They don't waste time. Every moment counts. Every choice is critical. Fruit flies don't live in the past or the future. They live in the present.

Fruit fly folks strive to love unconditionally. Fruit fly folks pursue their passions with blinders on.

Giving love and doing what they love is their path to peace and happiness.

If we're going to die one day, which seems to be the current trend for all living things, maximizing the warm feelings of peace and pure happiness for all parties involved should be our central ambition.

*(By the way, you just read the introduction.
I didn't call it the introduction because if
you're anything like me, you would
have just skipped right over it.)*

Decisions, Decisions, Decisions

S hould I leave my job? What color paint will look best in the foyer? Do I need the V-6 or will the four-cylinder be peppy enough? Should I call tonight or should I wait a couple of days so I don't seem too anxious? Am I in the mood for a salad? Where should I go on vacation? Will I look good in jeans or should I wear khakis?

Please allow me to shine the bright light of perspective on just about every "hard" decision you've been faced with. A few minutes before 9:00 AM on September 11, 2001, fathers and mothers and sons and daughters had mere seconds to choose between the guarantee of incineration or a desperate leap from the 80th floor.

As you know, this wasn't happening to soldiers in the heat of battle in some far off land. This wasn't happening during wartime at all. This was happening to New

Yorkers who, moments before, probably overpaid for a cup of coffee at Starbucks.

Yes, I do realize your day-to-day decisions are important. Yes, I know the horrific, no-win options available to those helpless folks in the Twin Towers on 9/11 in no way make your decision any clearer when considering if you should place your mom in a nursing home or when struggling to declare a major in college. I surely don't mean to devalue the circumstances of your life, as I am well aware of the butterfly effect in choice making.

And yes, I'm sure (and hope to God) you'll never find yourself at the heart of terrorist rage with your life on the line. That being said, your "big" decisions truly are big decisions.

However, as we all do while getting ready for work, Morty Frank probably mulled over upcoming big decisions as he brushed his teeth on the morning of September 11th. He became a victim at Ground Zero just a few hours after slipping his shoes on.

We went to high school together.

Like I just said, I'm sure (and hope to God) you'll never find yourself at the heart of terrorist rage with your life on the line. But you could.

Nothing is written in stone. No one is impervious to the tangled webs of life. Any of us could have been in Morty's shoes.

Next time you're hemming and hawing about a big decision, maybe you can remember Morty and his family and friends.

I would say: Try not to take too much time with decisions—but I don't need to. Because like it or not, we're running out of time just as fruit flies are.

In some cases, time ceases for us much quicker than we had bargained for. Whatever choice is on your plate, quickly collect all significant information and then just follow your gut. It won't lead you astray.

Live like a fruit fly.

Breadcrumbs

Your destiny is out there somewhere. It's playing a game of hide and seek with you. A game you may not win.

Your destiny could be a thousand miles away or it could just be around the corner. Regardless of its metaphysical distance, it will remain elusive.

Why is your destiny playing "hard to get"? Because it will not allow you to find it until you know exactly what it is you're looking for.

So what are you looking for? The answer is inside of you.

Hurry up, you're running out of time.

Once you have a clear picture of your destiny in your heart, declare that nothing will stop you from becoming a writer or a crossing guard or a lion tamer or a pediatric oncologist, and your destiny will hop on an airplane and move into your neighborhood.

So is it that easy? Does your destiny just come knocking on your door and hand you the keys to the circus or your own private practice? Of course not. Because honestly, it doesn't even know who you are yet.

So you hem and haw about wanting to fulfill your destiny and the both of you just go about your days, totally unaware of each other. Until one evening, you'll roll up your sleeves and say to yourself, "You know what, if I ever want to become a master of the pan flute like Zamfir, I better go out and buy a pan flute and maybe sign up for some lessons."

We'll now use split screen technology to see what your destiny is up to while you're getting into the car to head on over to the music store:

He's sitting on the couch in his boxer shorts and a T-shirt. Or maybe it's a she and she's sporting a matching bra and panty set. Whatever. In either case, he or she is eating a bowl of Honeycombs and watching *Miami Vice* reruns. The second you put the key into the ignition, your destiny pops up from the couch and gets dressed. You no longer need to search for it because it will find you.

How will it find you? I'm not sure how the universe fig-
ures it all out, and I have no idea how long it may take,
but your destiny will track you down like a bloodhound
as long as you leave a trail of breadcrumbs.

You drop breadcrumbs every time you remember to
have faith in your destiny.

You drop more breadcrumbs every time you successfully prevent negative thoughts and energy from
spreading doubt in your heart and mind.

You drop even more breadcrumbs every time you take
action toward your goal.

You don't have to quit your job or run away from home,
but if your heart won't be happy until you're a cartoon-
ist, you better start doodling with serious intentions.

Your destiny will eventually have you in its crosshairs.
If you're lucky, it will charge toward you and jump right
into your lap like a slobbering puppy. But more likely
than not, it will leave you a breadcrumb or two of its
own.

Your destiny's breadcrumbs can take many forms, so
be on the constant lookout like a focused lighthouse
keeper. Maybe you'll bump into your ex-girlfriend's previous ex-boyfriend and he'll unknowingly steer you to
your destiny. Maybe you'll be in the middle of a root
canal, and even though that suction thing is making its
deafening gurgling noise, you'll overhear the hygienist

talking to the receptionist about your destiny. Maybe you'll find breadcrumbs in your dreams. Maybe your destiny will send you a message in the subject line of a spam e-mail.

Keep your eyes, ears, and soul open. Follow all leads. Your destiny is closer than you think.

Live like a fruit fly.

"Destiny is no matter of chance.
It is a matter of choice: It is not a thing
to be waited for, it is a thing
to be achieved."
—William Jennings Bryan

A Quick Break Before
We Continue . . .

You might be sitting in a bookstore café somewhere, sipping an overpriced cappuccino or chai tea. Or you could be at home in bed reading a few pages before you conk out for the night. Or maybe you're on your lunch break sitting under a tree overlooking the parking lot. It's also quite possible that you're on the toilet. I don't want to know. Wherever you are, I'm sure you have breadcrumbs on the brain.

You might be inspired to start leaving them for your destiny ASAP.

Or maybe you have just made a pact with yourself to blindly follow the next trail of breadcrumbs you find. Don't regret it if you've ignored the signs thus far in exchange for "safer" routes. Today is a new day, and there's still time. But move quickly because the clock is ticking.

If you're like me, you've spent a lot of time reading motivational, inspirational, spiritual, philosophical, and metaphysical books. If so, you know that we've reached a critical juncture in this book. Either my book is going to start sucking like many others out there, or it's going to rise above the rest and go the extra mile.

Let's look at the last line of the preceding section: "Keep your eyes, ears, and soul open. Follow all leads. Your destiny is closer than you think."

I have to admit, those are some pretty profound words. But profound words come and go. I've read volumes of profound words, but I usually end up wanting to shout: "Where's your proof?!"

I knew long ago that one day I'd write this fruit fly book. I promised myself not to leave you, the reader, hanging. I won't light a flame under your butt with this bread-crumb concept without providing proof of its power. Flames of that nature are easily extinguished.

Just a side note: I also promised myself when I began writing this book not to make pithy references to the Star Wars or Matrix trilogies. So far so good, but as Yoda said in *The Empire Strikes Back* . . .

I almost slipped up.

Live like a fruit fly.

*"Every man has his own destiny:
the only imperative is to follow it,
to accept it, no matter where
it leads him."*

—Henry Miller

Breadcrumbs, Part Two
The Proof of Its Power

"AS FAR BACK AS I CAN REMEMBER, I ALWAYS WANTED TO BE A GANGSTER."

—*Henry Hill in* Goodfellas

A nd as far back as I can remember, I always wanted to be a writer.

To get his foot in the door with the mob, the young Henry Hill volunteered to carefully valet park cars for Cosa Nostra constituents.

What did I do early on to manifest my childhood dream? Nothing. Absolutely nothing. I wouldn't even pick up a pen or wait the fifteen minutes it took to boot up the good ol' Commodore 64.

Why should I even try to write? I'd ask myself. *I'll never be a Salinger, a Vonnegut, a Dalai Lama, or even a Judy Blume for that matter. What do I have to say to the world?*

I had a breakdown in Rob Leone's bedroom back in eleventh grade. We were sitting around, listening to Springsteen and daydreaming about how our futures may or may not unfold. I time-traveled to my postcollegiate life and, out of nowhere, my eyes got teary and clouded my vision. It was five years away, but I could feel the impending doom.

I was the Titanic heading for the Iceberg of Employment Misery.

So I lived out my days in high school and then in college watching the other kids make plans to be doctors, lawyers, corporate execs, and other assorted bigwigs. And I walked the halls as a non-writing wannabe writer.

And just as I prophesized back in the day with Rob, the iceberg was waiting for me in the dark of night.

I quit or was fired from sixteen jobs. Boy, were my parents proud. Not only did I have to deal with letting people down who expected great things from me, but I also was in a world of money trouble. You know the drill: living off credit cards, borrowing cash from friends and family, debt closing in on me from every angle.

Complaining is all I'd do to alleviate my sorrow. Sales and marketing wasn't for me. I just wanted to be a writer.

Many years have passed, but I remember this moment as if it took place only moments ago: I was standing outside the Long Island house where I grew up. My family was inside preparing Thanksgiving dinner, and I was bellyaching to a friend on the phone. She had always been compassionate, sympathetic, and accommodating to my bad-news-bear's mentality, but on that day, she totally snapped.

"That's it, Gabe. I'm not listening to this anymore! Just start writing and don't call me until you do."

"But what should I write about?" I whined.

I had much more to say, but she sternly silenced me with, "Anything. I don't care. Just write. Call me when you have something on paper."

And then she hung up.

I owe just about everything to her. If it weren't for her breadcrumbs, you'd be sitting on the toilet right now with yet another book that will leave you with the same unanswered questions.

When I finally clicked on the Microsoft Word icon on my desktop, I had absolutely no idea what to write. I rambled for a page or two . . . three hundred pages later, I was close to finishing my first manuscript. Then I wrote another.

The rejections started piling up. I was pissed and even depressed for a while because I felt like a total failure. But sitting here as I type to you now, I see the much larger picture.

Here's what happened behind the scenes:

I turned on my computer and launched Microsoft Word. My destiny raised his eyebrows and looked up from his bowl of Wheaties; he thought he heard a knock at the door. I stalled because I didn't know what to type so he went right back to watching the *Miami Vice* rerun. The moment my thoughts flowed from my mind to my fingers to the monitor, my destiny was already out the door following the path of breadcrumbs I was leaving behind.

Jump ahead a year: I was having breakfast at this little bohemian café in Miami's design district. There was a girl two tables away who looked incredibly familiar. She glanced up at me, but I looked away. I wasn't in the mood for any small talk or obligatory chitchat. A few moments later, she tapped my shoulder.

I was going to have breadcrumbs with my pancakes if I liked it or not.

It didn't take long for us to figure out that both of our parents' life savings was deposited in the University of Miami's bank account for the same four years.

It turns out that she was a professional journalist. I told

her that I was a writer too and that's when her whole demeanor changed. She kind of rolled her eyes; I'm guessing because she'd heard that from everyone and their mothers.

We talked for a couple of minutes more and then she ended our short encounter with, "Hey, it was good meeting you. You should send me some of your stuff."

She twirled away without offering me her card or e-mail address or anything.

My first instinct was to let her off the hook, but something inside made the following words flow from my mouth, "Do you have a card so I can send you some of my stuff?"

She begrudgingly dug through her bag for a card, handed me a wrinkled one, shot me a forced smiled, and scadoodled out of my life.

A few days later, I was staring at my unfinished book while deliberating if I should e-mail any of it to her. Honestly, her attitude, or what I perceived to be her attitude at the time, didn't jive with me, and I was on the verge of eighty-sixing her business card. Once again, something inside took control and didn't allow my infantile ego to get in the way.

I forwarded her a few pages of my meanderings. I knew she'd hate it, but at least I sent something and completed the circle.

Within an hour, she returned an e-mail. She loved my stuff. Actually, it's more accurate to say that she was *in love* with my stuff.

In the past, I'd walk by art galleries wondering if my writing, my art, was up to par with the pieces I'd see hanging in windows. I finally received the validation I'd been looking for from a *real* writer.

That would have been enough for me right there, but my destiny was out of breadcrumbs and was ready to jump into my lap.

My cell phone rang two weeks later. It was an editor from *The Miami Herald*. She called based on a strong recommendation made by the girl in the café.

For several years now, my column appears regularly in its paper—complete with my thumbprint-size head-shot, name, and e-mail address.

I made it.

I have to admit that my eyes just welled up a bit. You have no idea how miserable I was before this happened. Or maybe you do. It's painful to deny your destiny for so long. Nothing seems to work out right.

Keep your eyes, ears, and soul open. Follow all leads. Your destiny is closer than you think.

Live like a fruit fly.

P.S. I have a secret for you. I haven't told anyone until this very moment. Remember the time I wept in Rob Leone's room all of those years ago? I still knew, deep down, that it would all eventually work out. Somehow I just knew.

"I expect to pass through this life but once.
If therefore, there be a kindness I can show, or
any good thing I can do to any fellow being,
let me do it now, and not defer or neglect it,
as I shall not pass this way again."

—William Penn

Two Minutes Later

It's truly amazing. Once I knew to look for bread-crumbs, I found them all over the place, and I still do. I just turned on the TV and clicked around until I found George Carlin on *Inside the Actor's Studio*. He just said, "Massage your dreams. They'll come true."

A Question from the Audience ...

After I made a friend swear up and down that she wouldn't steal my idea (unpublished writers are always afraid someone's going to steal their work), I e-mailed her thirty pages of this book.

Her response: "*Who* chooses our destiny?"

Hmmm . . .

I'm not going to pretend I have the answer to this question. I mean, who am I to really know for sure?

However, I trust my instincts implicitly. After quieting my thoughts and peering into my heart, an answer was revealed and I have to be honest with you, it feels right on the money: We choose our destiny.

There isn't a doubt in anyone's mind that Robert Zimmerman was born with the *capacity* to become a lyrical genius. I believe that divine or universal intent was and is always at play.

Robert consciously or subconsciously followed a trail of breadcrumbs and became Bob Dylan.

But at the end of the day, it was his choice. He could easily have missed or ignored all the signs pointing the way as many people do. Instead of becoming a musical revolutionary and icon, he could have pursued a career in horticulture or garage door sales. Thankfully, Robert picked up a guitar and inspired millions of us.

Lew Alcindor was a pretty tall kid for his age. Regardless of the outside forces at play, it was his decision to become the NBA legend Kareem Abdul-Jabbar.

Jonas Salk . . .

Abraham Lincoln . . .

Nelson Mandela . . .

Neale Donald Walsch . . .

Bill Gates . . .

J. K. Rowling . . .

Muhammad Ali . . .

Barack Obama . . .

My parents . . .

Your parents . . .

Me . . .

You . . .

The list goes on and on, and it will continue to go on and on.

Breadcrumbs, once they are noticed, will never lead us down a damaging path if we choose to pick them up. But as you can surely deduce from the above list, your choice can affect many more people than just yourself.

Choose wisely. Regardless of what the Rolling Stones say, time isn't on your side.

Live like a fruit fly.

"It is not in the stars to hold our destiny but in ourselves."
—William Shakespeare

Scenes from
Return of the Jedi

Luke Skywalker and Obi-Wan Kenobi have a heart to heart on Dagobah:

Obi-Wan cuts to the chase with Luke and tells him that he can't escape his destiny. Facing Darth Vader again is something Luke must do. Luke knows this but also knows he can't kill his own father. Obi-Wan laments that if Luke won't fulfill his destiny, all is already lost.

Luke Skywalker turns himself over to Darth Vader:

Vader basically says, "Listen kid, Obi-Wan had similar silly thoughts. But neither of you nincompoops have any idea how cool the power of the Dark Side is. Regardless, I answer to the man."

Luke sort of replied, "Sorry Charlie. Over my dead body."

To which Vader said, and I'm paraphrasing, "Damn teenagers! Fine, have it your way if that's your destiny. Nice knowing you."

Luke Skywalker meets the Emperor:

Cocky and creepy as ever, the Emperor tells young Luke that he's in the same boat as his dad and there's nothing he can do about it. They're both just pawns in the Emperor's plans.

Luke and Vader duke it out and the duel ends with the senior Skywalker wheezing in defeat. The Emperor orders Luke to fulfill his destiny and finish off his father. Luke takes a breath, switches off his light saber, and says with divine confidence, "Never." (That always gives me goose bumps.)

Luke casts his light saber to the metallic ground and calmly explains that the Emperor has failed and that he is now a Jedi.

As we all know, Luke prevails.

Lots of talk about destiny here. Everyone thought they knew how it was going to unfold for Luke, but at the crescendo, he proved to be the one in charge of setting the course for his own destiny. Just like you can. Just as you will when the time is right.

That time is now.

Use the Force like a fruit fly.

*Destiny is no matter of chance.
It is a matter of choice: It is not a thing
to be waited for, it is a thing
to be achieved."*

—William Jennings Bryan

Breadcrumbs,
Part Three

Before we continue, please take a moment to look up the lyrics to Frank Sinatra's "My Way." I'll wait here until you get back.

Back already? C'mon, I know you didn't do it. At least promise me you'll search for it online later. Deal? Good.

So, the editor from the *Miami Herald* didn't just hand me the weekly column after the first time we spoke.

Wait . . .

I'll probably get shot in the back of the head for saying this, but I don't see what the big deal was all about with Sinatra. He had a good voice, but so did my chorus teacher in the third grade.

It just annoys me that he was so famous for so many songs that weren't even his own. I love the lyrics to "My Way," and it's very fitting for this chapter but Paul Anka is the guy who wrote the tune for Ol' Blue Eyes.

I'm going to start this section over . . .

Breadcrumbs,
Part Three (Take 2)

Before we continue, please take a moment to look up the lyrics to Paul Anka's "My Way." I'll wait here until you get back.

So, the editor from the *Miami Herald* didn't just hand me the weekly column after the first time we spoke.

Wait, wait, wait . . .

Paul Anka didn't really *write* this song either. He *rewrote* it. Three French guys by the names of Jacques Revaux, Gilles Thibaut, and Claude François originally dreamt it up.

It doesn't seem very fruit flyish to expend so much energy on such frivolities, but there is something to learn from this.

The lesson here is to give credit where credit is due.

I'm sure many of us have worked for bosses who have presented their employees' ideas as their own. I'm sure many of us are guilty of reading something or hearing something only to regurgitate it later in conversation as if we were the big brain behind the thought.

On face value, these are minor infractions. But I don't need to tell you that even the slightest dishonesty can come back to haunt you. Sometimes in ways you never dreamed possible in your worst nightmares. As the giant clock in the sky advances at an alarming rate, we're going to encounter real issues that aren't going to be very fun to deal with. Creating a possible crevice where more harmful issues may slide through is absolute lunacy.

Give credit where credit is due. If we strike when the iron is hot, we'll have our well-deserved day in the sun.

Live like fruit fly.

Breadcrumbs,
Part Three (Take 3)

Before we continue, please take a moment to look up the lyrics to Revaux's, Thibaut's, and François's "My Way." I'll wait here until you get back.

So, the editor from the *Miami Herald* didn't just hand me the weekly column after the first time we spoke. Our initial conversation went something like this:

"I heard you write like that John Cusack movie *High Fidelity*."

She didn't say anything after that. I guess she was waiting for me to confirm or deny what she heard.

I thought about it for a moment. If I agreed to that comparison, I'd come off sounding cocky. But maybe I'd appear unsure of my ability if I brushed off the compliment. I mean, *High Fidelity*—it's one hell of a smart flick.

Too much time elapsed, and the extended silence on the phone needed to be dealt with.

I finally said, "Yeah, I guess you can say I write like that. Honestly, I can jot down a thousand words about toilet paper, and by the end, you'd think we're best friends."

I went for extra cocky.

"So, I've been told you know a lot about the nightlife scene?"

"Of course," I was totally guilty of overinflating my knowledge, but this was sort of a job interview after all.

"You keep up with all of the local bands and new bars?"

"I go out all the time. I know the ins and outs." I'm not sure what I meant by "I know the ins and outs." It was just some nonsense that flowed from my mouth on its own accord.

"Well, even though she (the girl who force-fed me breadcrumbs at the bohemian café) vouched for you, we're going to ask that you write a mock piece for us. Just go out somewhere and write about it. If we like it, you'll be writing one of our nightlife columns."

Later that evening, equipped only with a pen and a geeky red notebook, I took a seat at a local jazz club and ordered a cup of coffee.

Between sets, I hobnobbed with the pianist, bassist, and drummer. When the trio returned to their musical meanderings and syncopations, I conducted interviews with the bartenders and patrons.

This was the first real writing assignment of my life, but it felt so natural, as if I were a seasoned veteran. It was my destiny, and I felt happy.

(It is my destiny and I feel happy.)

I got back to my apartment with pages and pages of scribbled notes.

After attempting to emulate the style of genuine journalists for a good two hours, I got up to take a break because the delete key on my laptop was seeing most of the action.

I paced around and considered throwing in the towel. I brilliantly b.s.'d my way through writing courses in college and couldn't figure out why I was having so much trouble faking it as a journalist. It should have been a no-brainer because the guy on piano was literally 95% blind and almost completely deaf. I had enough info on this extraordinary virtuoso to write a book.

The answer surfaced while noshing on a handful of peanuts.

The reason I was struggling to write eloquent, journalistic-sounding sentences worthy of a major newspaper was simply because I just wasn't a journalist. Nor did I even want to be a journalist.

But at the same time, I didn't want to blow my once-in-a-lifetime chance to be a published writer.

There were two clear-cut choices to decide between. Either I do the best at writing like a typical, but boring, newspaper guy (which would probably pull the wool over the eyes of *The Herald* and yield me the gig) or write the column using my chatty voice, which, of course, could always be relied upon to get a laugh out of my friends, but would almost certainly turn off the editors of a paper.

What to do, what to do. . . . Hours slipped by and the sun was getting ready to rise. It was then I remembered what Robert Frost had said about taking the road less traveled. . . .

I snubbed caution and wrote three hundred words about the hear-no-evil, see-no-evil piano player and the remaining five hundred words about the lack of sufficient air conditioning in the club that night.

The editors loved it, and my first column appeared in the following Friday's weekend section.

From the outside, it must look like I gambled with fulfilling my childhood dream. But I was absolutely convinced my breadcrumbs would only be found on the road less traveled. Choosing that path has made all the difference.

Don't be afraid to stick to your guns. As Sinatra, Anka, Revaux, Thibaut, and François suggested, do it your way. You'll be proud of yourself regardless of the outcome.

Live like a fruit fly.

"The saddest thing in life is wasted talent.
You can have all the talent in the world,
but if you don't do the right thing,
nothing happens."

—A Bronx Tale

Take 5

All work and no play makes Gabe a dull guy.
All work and no play makes Gabe a dull guy.

All work and no play makes Gabe a dull guy.
All work and no play makes Gabe a dull guy.
All work and no play makes Gabe a dull guy.

All work and no play makes Gabe a dull guy.
All work and no play makes Gabe a dull guy.
All work and no play makes Gabe a dull guy.
All work and no play makes Gabe a dull guy.
All work and no play makes Gabe a dull guy.

A crucial component of our fruit fly agenda is doing what we can to fulfill our destinies before we find ourselves pushing up daisies. But all work and no play will make us dull.

9/11 was a big wake up call for most of us. At any moment, it can all come to an end.

So why suffer through the drudgery of a thankless, unrewarding job? How dare we not devote almost every available moment to our quest of manifesting our deepest desires?

In that last sentence, please notice I used the word "almost." Pursue your passions with blinders on, but allow time for simple pleasures.

Call your sister so you can hear your nephews laughing in the background.

Go to the movies and munch on a big tub of popcorn.

Sit and listen in awe to "Kind of Blue" by Miles Davis.

Play footsies with your sweetie.

Shoot around on the basketball court with your buddies.

Look at old pictures while drinking a glass of chocolate milk.

Wake up early to see a sunrise.

Stay up really late just because you can.

I guarantee you'll come back to the trail of breadcrumbs feeling refreshed and even more focused.

I also guarantee not a single soul trapped in the Twin Towers had any thoughts that even resembled, "I wish I had one more day on this earth so I could just make a few more sales calls."

Live like a fruit fly.

Fight for Your Write

Maybe it's connected to the dumbing down of America or maybe it's because she thinks I'm dumb; but from time to time, my editor at the paper has a field day with her red pen.

As Bobby Brown would say, "That's her prerogative." But when she makes an error or defunnifies one of my jokes or waters down my wit, I'm the one who looks . . . well, dumb.

I have to hold myself back from ripping her a new one in an e-mail. When I'm right, she should know when she's wrong.

But my destiny taps me on the shoulder and advises me otherwise. My destiny reminds me how quickith this can all be taken awayith.

If I opened my fat mouth just to prove I'm right, she'd still have the last laugh and may decide to relieve me of my column. Then I'd just be a guy who used to write for a big newspaper. And then maybe this book wouldn't have gotten published. Which of course means you wouldn't be reading it right now.

It's more beneficial for all parties involved if I refrain from sending that scathing e-mail and follow the advice of John and Paul: Let it be.

I don't have any proof of this, but if you ruin everything you worked for by foolishly needing to be right, your destiny may become stingy with its breadcrumbs. Because of this, I remember instead to appreciate my editor because she's the one who gave me my big break into the writing world to begin with.

There are times you must desperately fight like Ali versus Frazier to prove you're right. But times like these are few and far between. Don't second-guess yourself when your heart tells you to hang up your boxing gloves.

The end is getting closer with every sunset. Pay attention when your destiny taps you on the shoulder.

Live like a fruit fly.

4:37AM

If you're only going to read one part of this book, serendipity has brought you to the precise page.

I just got home from my bartending gig a couple of minutes ago. My brain is running on fumes because I'm so exhausted, but I feel compelled to write this chapter before the sun makes itself known.

Quick backstory: Even though I got my big break as a nightlife columnist, I had to keep my bleak corporate job because, well, I still needed to eat and pay rent.

Since I was out on the town all the time gathering info for my nightlife column, I'd watch the amount of money passing through the hands of bartenders with envy. To make a short story shorter, I took my last $400 and enrolled in bartending school.

I scored three shifts at one of the bars I'd written about, and the money I pull in from pouring drinks is more than enough to make ends meet. I love bartending because my job is to make people laugh and feel good.

Anyway, the bar was jam-packed tonight and once again, as I ran around like a maniac attempting to keep everyone smiling, the other bartender was moving at half-speed because he knew I wouldn't let a single tipping customer fall through the cracks.

As I poured drinks and cleared tables, I role-played the conversation I was going to have with him at the end of the night. I planned responses to everything he might retaliate with and this mental process alone was enough to further fuel my anger. Plus, I cracked a tooth on an apple earlier in the day and a jagged sliver of enamel was carving a divot into my tongue. I wasn't a happy camper at all.

There's a forty-year-old guy who owns the bar around the corner and he comes into my place from time to time to borrow a bottle or to have a quick belt of booze. He's always happy and extremely humble and generous. But tonight he looked like he just saw a ghost. Actually, it's more accurate to say he himself looked like a ghost. Like his wind was knocked out or his life was drained from his soul.

His brother died in a car accident a few minutes before, and he just didn't know what to do or where to go. I didn't know what to say so I just gave him a hug.

The night before, he celebrated the tenth anniversary of his bar with a huge soirée and was worried about the $2,200 he had to quickly shell out to fix his ice machine.

And now nothing matters anymore. His perpetual peaceful smile has been replaced by an expression that I can only describe as horror. Utter horror.

In an instant, everything changes.

But I'm not telling you anything you don't already know. We've all been to funerals. We've all seen or felt the horror.

I'm just here to remind you. In an instant, you can be blindsided with news that will turn your world upside down and inside out and then all you'll be left with are memories and missed opportunities.

Smile. Unless you're faced with true horror, nothing is as bad as it seems.

Live like a fruit fly.

Is It Safe?

I went to the dentist this morning to take care of the broken tooth responsible for the lacerations on my tongue.

First the bad news: I have to go back Thursday for a root canal. Then, my tooth needs to be built up for a post and a crown. It's going to cost $1,400 out-of-pocket.

Now for the good news: There isn't any.

After the dentist gave me a feeble handshake, I was directed into a cubbyhole of an office where I was flashed the phoniest of smiles from a plump lady wearing huge Sally Jesse Rafael glasses.

She handled me with the finesse of a finance manager at an exotic car dealership and treated me as if I had no business even being there. She was so syrupy and patronizing. I was going to say something like, "You can save this transparent routine for someone who isn't worlds more intelligent than you." But I just kept my mouth shut because I wanted to get the hell out of there.

Fourteen hundred bucks! Do you know how many CDs I can buy with that kind of cash? And now I have to piss it away to fix my tooth.

Speaking of CDs, I got home from the dentist with a tongue that's still being carved like a Thanksgiving turkey. I just wanted to listen to this John Legend album I recently picked up but I couldn't find it anywhere.

I really started to go mental looking for it. Like Godzilla in Tokyo, I violently flipped over everything that wasn't nailed down in my place. Now I have to respend money to replace this CD on top of draining my savings account to send my dentist's kids to prep school.

I was rapidly losing my cool in the quicksand of negativity.

I turned on my computer to screw around on the Internet in an effort to calm down a bit. I went to CNN.com and was subsequently baptized in the waters of perspective.

Dozens of people were killed and hundreds of others were wounded in a horrific terrorist attack in London.

So let me rewind back to the beginning of this chapter:

First the bad news: I have to go back Thursday for a root canal. Then, my tooth needs to be built up for a post and a crown. It's going to cost $1,400 out-of-pocket.

Now for the good news: as I said in the last chapter, unless you're faced with true horror, nothing is as bad as it seems.

The waters of perspective have reminded me to appreciate all that is good in my world. My family, my health (minus one tooth), and so on and so forth.

If you're reading these words now, there's a good chance you weren't slaughtered across the pond today as you innocently scrambled just to get to work on time. I'm sure you have plenty to appreciate. It's all about proper perspective.

Life is too short to dwell on the trivial.

Live like a fruit fly.

Active Appreciation

Sometimes I find myself feeling gloomy for absolutely no reason. I could be checking my e-mail or chomping on a bowl of Cocoa Pebbles or driving to the bookstore and there I am, frowning like the world is coming to an end.

Well, to be honest, of course there's some sort of reason for the sad puss on my face. I might have been thinking about how cute my ex-girlfriend looked right after she fell asleep. Maybe I was swept over by a wave of homesickness. It could have been a million other reasons.

If I were a "normal" person, I'd unconsciously allow my runaway, negative thoughts to be commander-in-chief of my emotions until my mind found the next distraction.

But what do *I* do? I get angry with myself because I should know better.

A fruit fly would savor a bowl of Cocoa Pebbles, possibly its last bowl of excessively sweetened cereal, with a smile on its face.

So there I am, upset at something I temporarily have no control over. I then thrash myself for being a hypocrite because of this fruit fly book. Now the fun starts—the negativity begins to compound:

I run out of milk. My friend calls five minutes later and leaves me yet another annoying message about his upcoming wedding. And then I turn on the news and some town in the Midwest is on fire or being washed over in a flood. And then I see on the Web that another dozen people were blown to bits.

And before you know it, it seems like the world really *is* coming to an end.

That's when I pull Active Appreciation out of my bag of tricks. It's a simple process that works like a charm. When you catch yourself feeling like the sky is falling, take control of your thoughts.

WAIT!

DON'T SAY IT!

I DON'T WANT TO HEAR ANY BELLYACHING ABOUT HOW HARD IT IS TO CONTROL YOUR THOUGHTS!

Just wrestle them to the ground! Overpower them! Don't forfeit your authority! You are the master of your mind!

Sorry to yell, but I've just about lost all patience for the typical whiney response of, "It's too hard. It's not as easy as you think."

My retort to that is blah, blah-blah, blah, blah.

I'll agree it isn't easy, but with laser-guided focus, people have figured out how to split the atom. Others successfully landed on the moon. Cancer patients, a few short steps from Death's door, willed their cells to rejuvenate. And there are those who survived constant torture in concentration camps. Don't tell me it's too hard to briefly claim responsibility for your scattered thoughts.

"BUT GABE, HOW DO I DO IT? I'm not a Buddhist monk or a yogi, or a spiritual guru. I just don't know where to start. Please help."

I might suggest you go buy a book on meditation to learn how, and leave me alone. I might be one of those authors who tells you to do something without explaining how. Fortunately, I'm not that guy.

Active Appreciation *is* the how and the way.

Step one: Take a deep breath. Then breathe out fully. Next, return to normal respiration as controlled for your convenience by your parasympathetic nervous system.

If you have successfully completed the first step, congratulations! You're not dead. I say this lightheartedly, but in all seriousness, millions upon millions of earth's inhabitants are dying as we speak. As the first step confirmed, you are not one of them, so let's move on:

Step two: Sometimes it helps me to close my eyes. If you're driving a car or operating heavy machinery after chugging cough medicine, I recommend skipping this step.

Step three: Say to yourself, "Thank you." And I don't mean you should just silently and unconnectedly say it in your mind. Instead, with concentrated intention, say "thank you" directly to yourself. Literally, earnestly, and warmly thank yourself for bringing you to that precise moment. Your current situation might not be ideal, but I have absolutely no doubt you overcame all odds to get to where you are. It is the present moment, the only possible moment, and therefore, the perfect moment.

Step four: Thank yourself for remembering to use Active Appreciation before you spiraled too far down into a dreadful mental abyss.

Step five: Laugh at the pathetically flimsy negative thoughts barraging your brain. Within a few minutes, they'll be powerless.

Step six: Mentally step away from negative thoughts. Of course they'll still be there, but they're no longer any of your concern. Then, as if your life depends on it (because it really does), focus every ounce of energy you can possibly muster on sending out appreciation and gratitude from each cell of your body.

The only thoughts you're concerned with now are those of thanks. If it helps, visualize waves of appreciation shooting out of your mind like lightning bolts as a direct effect of your bidding. If it helps, keep saying, "Thank you, thank you, thank you, thank you . . . " over and over again in your mind. Say it out loud if need be.

What are we thanking the universe for? For everything that has happened, is happening, and is about to happen. Send thanks in advance for all of the good coming your way from right around the corner. Do this with faith and smile as you see fortune manifesting not too far down the road.

What's that you say? It's not working? Maybe you should reread step six. I'll wait for you here until you're done.

Okay, you're back. But you're still saying it's not getting the job done. You're probably overlooking or not paying enough attention to the most important part of step six. Since we're running out of time, I'll highlight it for you: send out appreciation and gratitude AS IF YOUR LIFE DEPENDS ON IT (BECAUSE IT REALLY DOES).

You may or may not agree, but I believe our lives are the product of our thoughts. If I am right, your life really is depending upon this. If I am right, which I know I am, sending out appreciation to castrate negativity is just as critical as avoiding a lethal cobra strike. If I am wrong, which I know I'm not, use Active Appreciation anyway because it works—even if its only function is to take your mind off things for a while. But trust me, this process has the power to quicken the return of your smile, alter your reality, and help get you where you want to be.

Now that we're all on the same page, here's the travel-size version of Active Appreciation:

Step one: Breathe

Step two: Send sincere thanks.

Live like a fruit fly.

Is It Safe? Part Two

The dentist collected all the instruments in the office and proceeded to stick them in my mouth at the same time. Drills, suction tubes, scrapers, pokers, needles, gauze pads, plastic wedges, and fingers on top of fingers stretched my jaw to the limit. At one point, I'm pretty sure I noticed a few #2 pencils being shoved in there for good luck.

The root canal procedure lasted about two hours. The cute little dentist said the reason why it took so long was because I'm a tall guy and I have very long tooth roots. I was about to make a sophomoric joke about my size-12 shoes, but I spared her my perverted comedic styles because my damn mouth was too sore to form words.

I'm home now, and besides the fact that it feels as if Bruce Lee gave me one of his lightening quick jabs to the face, I'm doing relatively well.

The point of this section isn't to vent to you or dig for sympathy because it's only a root canal and not the end of the world.

I just wanted to share something my dentist said when I initially sat down in the chair.

She explained the procedure step by step, and I sarcastically interrupted with, "Sounds like the two of us are in for a lot fun."

She smiled because she knew I was just joking. She then added, "Well, it's probably not going to be much fun for you, but it will be for me."

"This is fun for you?" I asked with a disbelieving smirk.

"I love doing root canals. It's my art. If I didn't love it, I wouldn't be standing here right now."

You spend a majority of your life at work. Whether you love what you do for a living or hate what you do for a living, your world, as you know it, will one day come to an end.

Maybe it won't be your time to go for many, many years. But then again, maybe your number will be called tomorrow. The question is this: if you don't love what you do or, even worse, are miserable on a daily basis, how much longer are you going to allow yourself to be stuck like this? Because, I got news for you friend, you're going to die.

Did you let those last four words marinate in your brain? I know it sucks. I know you don't want to think about it, but . . .

You're going to die.

I know you may have family depending on you and you don't want to let anyone down. But you have a right to your happiness and you must fight to find it. You must fight with everything you got. No-rules street fighting. Because you are going to die, and I guarantee that the pain of regret will eclipse any pain you're experiencing now.

Once again, for the cheap seats, you are going to die, and I guarantee that the pain of regret will eclipse any pain you're experiencing now.

Live like a fruit fly.

"Without passion man is a mere latent force and possibility, like the flint which awaits the shock of the iron before it can give forth its spark."

—Henri Frédéric Amiel

Clown School

"The best thing about the future is that
it comes only one day at a time."

—*Abraham Lincoln*

But . . .

"You hear that, Mr. Anderson? That is the sound
of inevitability. It is the sound of your death."

—*Agent Smith to Neo in* The Matrix

And with that being said . . .

I know you feel passionate about your passions. And
I'm sure you're going to tend to them as soon as that
delicious day comes when you don't have as much to
juggle. You have your job, bills, friends, love life (or lack

thereof), maybe a minivan full of kids, maybe a sick uncle, and so on.

Unfortunately, for most of us, that day isn't going to come anytime soon. The only time we find ourselves with almost nothing to juggle is when we're too old to juggle for ourselves anymore.

You're going to have to become a better juggler. Right now.

Live like a fruit fly.

Utter Horror

It's such a cliché, but the truth is, life goes on. Less than a week after his brother died in an automobile accident, that guy I told you about on page 44 was back at his bar serving drinks and doing his best to smile. It's obvious that the sparkle was gone from his eyes, and it kills me to see him scouring over the police report from the accident but . . . life must go on.

I was clicking back and forth from channel to channel, just as I'm sure you were, on the morning of September 11. One of the news stations showed one of the Towers crumbling. The next station focused on the other Tower struggling to remain on its feet. I had to click past a cooking show and then past Barney singing a little song to a bunch of kids to find a shot of the Pentagon on fire.

Through tears, I clicked back to Barney.

It was the most surreal moment of my life. As my beloved hometown and country was under attack, a purple dinosaur entertained children just as the TV guide said it would.

There was a lesson in the middle of the horror: for those not directly involved, life, regardless of the situation, has no choice but to go on.

For those of us privileged enough to experience a brand-new day, we're confronted with a choice: Do we live helplessly consumed by sorrow and self-pity? Or are we going to sandblast our current situation to uncover the silver lining?

For the guy who owns the bar, and for Morty Frank's family and close friends, and for the millions of people currently dealing with such loss all over the planet, your lack of interest in the silver lining is understandable. But I have a feeling your departed loved ones would implore you to find your smile again. Because I'm sure that's what you would wish for them.

Keep wiping your tears, carry the torch, and set off on a quest for the silver lining. You'll definitely find it if you allow yourself to look. You'll definitely find it if you dig far enough. Dig to China if you must. You owe it to them and you owe it to yourself.

Live like a fruit fly.

The Opposite of Utter Horror and the Generosity of a Stranger

10:54 AM: A few minutes ago, I had the privilege of witnessing a once-in-a-lifetime event. Only a couple of hundred people on the planet were able to see what I just saw. Maybe a few folks were lucky enough to catch it in times past, but I seriously doubt it. Maybe it will happen again in the future but chances are slim.

Ready?

I was just fortunate enough to see, with my own two eyes, the successful launch of the space shuttle *Discovery*.

Big deal you say? *Big whoop?*

Allow me to clarify: I'm writing this chapter, via my laptop, as I'm flying home to visit my family in New York for a couple of days.

Yes. Now you get it. From the eighteenth row of a Jet-Blue airplane, I caught a glimpse of *Discovery* as it made its way to the heavens.

This isn't a big deal in itself, but it's a super-big whoop because as I'm sure you remember, on February 1, 2003, the space shuttle *Columbia* disintegrated upon reentry. Obviously, the seven astronauts aboard were killed. Needless to say, everyone on the plane today, as well as everyone on the planet, was holding his or her breath.

The captain said that we'd be able to see the launch from the right, or starboard side of the plane. Of course my seat was on the left, or port side, so I had to run back and forth through the isle like a maniac trying to become an eyewitness to history.

The starboard people were hogging up all of the good views, and I felt just like a little boy because all I wanted was one little peak.

I was about to give up and return to my seat, but a female baby boomer noticed me pouting. She said, "I already had a chance to see it. I'll get up so you can see."

Because of the generosity of a stranger, I now have a story to tell my grandkids.

Assuming, of course, my kids want to have kids. Assuming, of course, I have kids of my own. Assuming, of course, I get married. Assuming, of course, I ever have a girlfriend again. Okay, maybe I can forget about the grandkids thing, but at least I have a great story to share with you.

It took almost no effort for this woman to forgo her seat; but this little thoughtful gesture allowed me to see . . . well, one of the coolest things ever and I'll remember it forever.

We forget that all of our words and actions, as innocuous as they may seem at the time, affect the people and world around us.

We can easily be the catalyst to a lasting smile. But we can just as easily leave a scar or reopen an old wound.

Be mindful of all your thoughts, words, and deeds.

Generosity with your love, money, time, wit, bread-crumbs, or airplane seats clearly benefits those around you. And it's nice just to be nice.

But fruit flies will always do the right thing for another reason. They simply don't have time to deal with the consequences of reacting negatively. With each breath, the inevitable closes in. Fruit flies instinctively choose to be the source of another's smile simply because it keeps their path clear of mental obstacles. When they buzz away from an encounter, they'll feel no guilt nor dwell over anything upsetting. A fruit fly wouldn't even imagine leaving a scar on another because they know that scar would quickly become their own. There's so much to do and so little time.

The road ahead is rocky enough without creating your own obstacles.

And it's nice just to be nice.

Live like a fruit fly.

Time-Saving Tip #1

Turn off your TV. You've seen enough. By now, we know how every show ends:

The wacky roommates will kiss and make up before the closing credits.

The killer will be caught.

The motorcycle will be completed in the nick of time.

Hitler commits suicide in the bunker, and the Nazis lose the war.

The cheetah is the fastest land animal and unknowingly uses its tail for balance.

One of the two teams playing will definitely lose but both will take it far too seriously.

In local news: The anchorperson will stretch like a yoga master to make some sort of connection between a national story and (INSERT YOUR TOWN HERE). After the commercial break, you'll learn that the high school football coach in (INSERT YOUR TOWN HERE) was fired for doing something stupid like punching a kid or flirting with a cheerleader, and it's causing the teachers' union to meet with some other group.

National newscast: Michael Jackson's death still raises eyebrows. People were killed in the Middle East. Reporters everywhere will fail to ask politicians the tough questions.

Precious hours of your life flushed down the toilet.

Since I'm just as guilty, I'll have to admit my addiction to reruns of *The West Wing.* Sometimes you can't tear me away from a Lakers game. I can spend an entire night with *American Chopper*, The History channel, and Animal Planet. Then, of course, there's nothing better than holding hands with your main squeeze while you flick back and forth between Comedy Central and *Iron Chef*.

I'm going to pull back the reins on this TV tirade some more and say: I'm well aware that after a stressful day at the office, plopping down on the couch in front of the tube is like a visit to a decompression chamber. It allows you to virtually break away from "reality" for a bit.

HOWEVER . . . I can almost guarantee you that work will suck tomorrow just as bad as it sucked today. It's all the justification you'll need to allow yourself yet another evening of total devotion to the television.

When you wake up the next morning, you'll once again have to deal with your boss with chronic halitosis or your demanding clients or a classroom full of screaming third graders with speech problems. You'll get home, grab the remote and some Hot Pockets, and before you know it, it's ten years later.

You don't remember the last time you baked cookies for your kids. *Or* your significant other is fantasizing about cheating on you for myriad reasons. *Or* you haven't been to the gym in ages because you "just don't have the time." *Or* your dog is lethargic because you haven't played with him since he was a puppy. *Or* you've been putting off calling your grandma. *Or*, even worse, you haven't pursued your passion in eons.

Going back to what I said a few paragraphs before: Unless you're out saving the world during the day, precious hours of your life are being flushed down the toilet. And going way back to the opening of this book, where Muhammad Ali said, "At night when I go to bed, I ask myself, 'If I don't wake up tomorrow, would I be proud of how I lived today?'"

Turn off the TV.

Live like a fruit fly.

A Quick,
Lighthearted Break . . .

It was recently discovered that fruit flies carry a gene that allows them to develop a tolerance to alcohol. They appropriately named this gene the "hangover" gene. A doctor at some university released these findings, and I just read about it on the Internet.

I'm not sure if this applies to anything we're talking about here, but I got a kick out of it.

Live like a fruit fly and designate a driver.

Another Quick Break . . . Not Lighthearted, but Full of Heart

It's 2:26 AM and I just finished watching *March of the Penguins*. It is one of the most beautiful movies I've ever seen.

On the surface it's visually breathtaking, and the score is absolutely calming. But you need to *be* with this movie. Don't watch it with your mind. Feel it with your heart.

March of the Penguins is an eighty-four-minute massage for your soul.

It's also an eighty-four-minute message for your soul. And the message is this:

Love is all there is.

We're really not all too different from penguins. We're born, we grow up, and then fight to survive. We search for a mate, start a family, and sacrifice everything for our children.

Penguins have the same agenda.

Thankfully, we humans have figured out the basic survival thing; but, because of this, we've lost touch with the message. To fill the gaps of free time, we stress about 401Ks and the price of gas. We idolize celebrities and literally crucify our messengers who attempt to bring us back to the message.

Thankfully, you can't crucify a movie.

Schedule a massage for yourself today.

Don't put it off.

Don't count on tomorrow.

Live like a penguin.

Ponce de León

I'm not a geriatric specialist. I'm not even a doctor. Nor do I play one on TV. And now that I think about it, I can't remember the last time I've been to a doctor.

Hippocratic Oath or not, I'm going to write you a prescription for your mental and physical health:

Stay young.

That's it. That's all you need to know. Good luck. Take care.

Live like a fruit fly.

Ponce de León,
Part Two

What?

Was the prescription unclear?

Take 1 (one) tablet of Stay Young as soon as you awake and take 1 (one) tablet of Stay Young at bedtime. Liberally use as needed throughout the day. Keep out of reach of children since they do not need to be reminded of their youth.

Live like a fruit fly.

Ponce de León,
Part Three

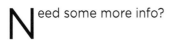eed some more info?

Okay, I have a box of Stay Young right here on my desk. I'm opening it up . . . taking out that piece of paper sandwiched in with the pills . . . unfolding it . . .

Here's what it says:

Prescribing Information:

Old age starts its siege against your cells the moment you decide to let it.

Yes, my dear friends, you consciously choose to get old.

You don't think so? Allow me to explain . . . I mean, allow me to keep reading:

With each capitulation to adulthood, the body and mind grow weaker. With each suppression of an innocent and instinctive reaction, youth fades. With each denial of an urge from the pure child inside, the distance from peace increases and the distance to the ultimate end decreases.

Take 1 (one) tablet of Stay Young as soon as you awake and take 1 (one) tablet of Stay Young at bedtime. Liberally use as needed throughout the day.

Now for a story from thirty-one years ago:

One day in the first grade, my teacher looked up at the clock, abruptly stopped herself in midthought, and instructed the class to put on our jackets.

She escorted us, single file, to the soccer field. The whole school was already there. Both fifth grade classes along with the science teacher were huddled around brown folding lunch tables that were dragged out for this mysterious occasion. I stepped out of line to get a closer look. Just as my teacher noticed I'd broken formation, I caught a glimpse of what was going on. The lunch tables were lined with model rockets and the fifth graders, who seemed, at the time, to be as old as M.I.T. grads, were busy tinkering with wires and miniature rocket engines.

The students as well as the teachers, some who were probably younger than I am now, were shooed back to a safer distance by the gym teacher. The fifth graders put on their safety goggles and successfully launched their rockets into the heavens (at least well past the tallest tree).

I was completely blown away by the *phhhhhtt* sound during takeoff and equally enthralled by the calm descent provided by small parachutes.

For us first graders, this was our inaugural experience with Waverly Park School's Aerospace Day. From that moment on, I couldn't wait for the years to pass until I reached the big-man-on-campus status and had a chance to sport safety goggles.

Twenty-seven years ago:

I'm in fifth grade and it's Aerospace Day.

I was already quite jaded by the school system and the little catty cliques so I wanted nothing to do with anything organized. I stood on the sidelines with my hands in my pockets like a mini James Dean while my classmates emulated NASA engineers.

I heard a deep rumble overhead, so I looked up and saw a 747. I literally lost my breath and couldn't even make a sound to alert my friends. It wasn't just your typical 747 schlepping people to Miami for suntans. This one was giving a piggyback ride to the space shuttle. Honestly, my heart is palpitating now just by remembering the details.

I was in awe. The moment was literally majestic. I saw a *real* spaceship in *real* life with my own eyes. I loved the experience and remember telling my friends how much I loved it (and I'm sure they responded with, "If you love it than why don't you marry it?").

As you know from page 63, while flying in a Jet Blue airplane en route to JFK, I saw the space shuttle *Discovery*.

Society dictates a thirty-seven-year-old must not react like a ten-year-old. We must hold back some emotions or face judgment.

I'm not going to sit here and say that I'm impervious to these expectations. When the captain first instructed us to look out the right side of the plane, I attempted to play it cool. I only let myself become mildly interested. And you know what? I felt like a big phony.

That fifth grader is still inside of me. Part of me will never grow up. And honestly, I hope I never cease to be amazed by stuff that wowed me when I was a kid.

I actually made a conscious decision to permit myself to feel whatever my body wanted to feel without worrying about acting the way I was "supposed" to feel. Seconds before that lady, that angel, allowed me to squeeze into her row to catch a glimpse, I paced up and down the isle in a panic. That innocent panic of possibly missing out . . . well, it felt like home.

When I saw the huge smoke plume in the wake of *Discovery*, I was looking out of the same eyes as the ten-year-old who saw it piggybacked on the 747. And I was equally, or even more so, in awe. It felt like home.

Kowtowing to the judgment of others is killing us. And although this may sound redundant, giving in to growing old is also killing us as well. You can slow down the dying process by choosing to stay young. Keep your ties to your youth. Act silly sometimes. Create something just to create. Shake with excitement. Smile. Don't hold everything inside. You're going to die one day. Don't help the process along.

Ponce de León failed to find the fountain of youth. He failed because he chose to look for it in Florida rather than looking inside himself.

I'll "read" it to you once again:

With each capitulation to adulthood, the body and mind grow weaker. With each suppression of an innocent and instinctive reaction, youth fades. With each denial of an urge from the pure child inside, the distance from peace increases and the distance to the ultimate end decreases.

Remember to Stay Young as soon as you awake and remember to Stay Young at bedtime. Liberally use as needed throughout the day.

Live like a fruit fly.

Bulletproof Vest

"FAITH IS THE STRENGTH BY WHICH A SHATTERED
WORLD SHALL EMERGE INTO THE LIGHT."

—*Helen Keller*

My brother-in-law's mom has a brain tumor.

She had one surgically removed last year and endured
the whole chemotherapy thing, but a new growth was
just discovered the other day. Her balance was a bit off
the last few weeks, and I think she subsequently fell a
few times. I'm sure she didn't want to confront the possibility of hearing unbearable news again, but a visit to
the doctor was obviously necessary. Maybe she'll beat
this thing; but then again, maybe it will beat her.

Our two families aren't as hopeful this time around, but nevertheless, I'll keep the faith.

Speaking of faith, I'm quite intrigued by my varying levels of it. The further removed a person is from me, the easier it is to be full of faith. But it might be more difficult for me to eliminate the needless worry and remain faithful if an immediate family member or I faced a challenge that required a miracle.

[soul searching]

[soul searching]

[soul searching]

Now that I've peered deep inside and let myself really think about this, I have faith that my faith will be rock solid even in the most horrific of situations. Because, when it comes down to it, sincere faith is really your only ally when circumstances are out of your control. And just like The Force in *Star Wars,* a powerful ally faith is.

Hopefully, my introspection into this subject will just turn out to be a mental exercise, and I'll never need to prove it to myself.

[thinking . . .]

[thinking . . .]

[thinking . . .]

Consider the bulletproof vest. If you're a cop, you won't have to rely on it every day, but it will save your life if you happen to get caught in the line of fire. But if you're not already wearing a vest when the bullets start to fly, it's not going to be so easy to locate one in the nick of time.

Fruit flies understand that faith operates like a bullet-proof vest. Fruit flies put one on every morning as soon as they wake up. Fruit flies constantly connect with faith even when they're surrounded by peace. Fruit flies know that by exercising faith every day, it can save them, their loved ones, and the planet in a time of crisis.

Because when the bullets of life begin to whiz by, which they no doubt will, it might be too late to start digging around for faith if you never tried it on for size before.

Connect with your faith today.

Live like a fruit fly.

"Faith is to believe what you do not yet see;
the reward for this faith is to see what you believe."
—Saint Augustine

Green Grass

I've been super stressed about this topic since I began to write this book.

Honestly, I was hoping I'd be able to avoid dealing with it.

But now I feel obligated to confront it because if I were in your shoes after reading the last section, I'd want me, the author, to have the guts to address what would normally be overlooked in similar books.

But honestly, I'm not sure if I can . . .

Okay . . . I just caught myself stalling . . . I guess there's no getting used to the cold water . . . I need to just jump in . . .

To quote the previous section: "Connect with your faith today."

What the hell am I talking about?

Faith in what exactly?

Do I mean faith in a divine presence?

Do I mean faith in the power of unconditional love?

Do I mean faith in oneself?

Yes, yes, and yes.

For those of you who already wear the bulletproof vest of faith, I obviously don't need to explain any of this to you.

For those of you who chalk everything up to coincidence and do not feel a connection to a God or a higher power or in the spiritual link of all things . . . well, there's no way you'd even get this far into the book. So if you are reading these words right now and consider yourself to be a complete atheist, I have news for you: you're actually sitting on the fence of faith.

For those of you on the fence: don't fret. Sometimes I'm right there with you. But so were Jesus and the Buddha, so we're in some pretty good company.

If it were a simplistic task to have faith all day, to *be* faith all day, our planet would be filled with billions of metaphysical masters.

But here we find ourselves on the fence. Regardless of our level of faith or belief in the divine, six feet of earth will one day envelop us. But in the meantime, I'm working on taking the plunge to the side of the fence where faith is absolute. I know in my heart that's where peace resides and life is too short to not strive for it.

I find myself hanging out with Buddha often, but my goal is to become more of a permanent resident of his side of the fence.

The question now is how . . . and this is the subject that has been intimidating me. I wish I could avoid tackling it, but I know I must. I can taste the breadcrumbs. Like Luke, I must face Vader. It's my path off the fence.

(Sorry for another Star Wars reference but you have to admit, I've kept it to a minimum.)

How do you keep the faith? You fake it until you make it.

It's honestly that simple.

Do you feel as if you don't have enough faith in a divine presence? Act as if you do.

Do you feel as if you don't have enough faith in unconditional love? Act as if you do.

Do you feel as if you don't have enough faith in yourself? Act as if you do.

Be loving in all situations. Walk through life as you'd imagine Moses or Mohammed or Jesus would. Always have room in your heart for forgiveness. Don't hope for best-case scenarios to present themselves, know they will.

Keep "pretending" you have faith, but do it from the bottom of your heart. When the time is right, absolute faith, just like your destiny, will one day jump into your lap and become one with you.

Maybe I'm wrong about this. But I really don't think so. And if I am, that's okay. I'll figure out how to get to the other side of the fence or will die trying.

Please give this a shot for yourself before you dismiss it. Time is running out for all parties involved.

Live like a fruit fly.

"I have one life and one chance to make it count for something . . . I'm free to choose what that something is, and the something I've chosen is my faith. Now, my faith goes beyond theology and religion and requires considerable work and effort. My faith demands—this is not optional—my faith demands that I do whatever I can, wherever I am, whenever I can, for as long as I can with whatever I have to try to make a difference."

—Jimmy Carter

"Don't Let the Sun Catch You Crying"

I found out about my brother-in-law's mom from my parents. They were discussing it in the car while I was sitting in the backseat (feeling like a little kid).

As soon as they were finished with this morbid topic, they transitioned to another one. I tried to tune it out, but I couldn't help but overhear them chatting it up about their friend's father. He's ninety-something years old and needs a pacemaker and is in a nursing home and so on and so forth.

Of course it's sad, but the chain reaction of mental extrapolating it caused in my head gave me that clenched-stomach feeling you'd get from leaning back too far in a chair.

My parents are going to be old one day. And that day is getting closer. For the most part, they still act young and are pretty healthy but . . . well, you know. The inevitable is inevitable.

And then I'll be having a discussion about them with either my sister or my wife (if I ever find one, or if one ever finds me).

Birthdays will be celebrated, old calendars will need to be replaced; and then before you know it, someone will be having that discussion about me.

By the way, I was sitting in the backseat of my parent's car because I was visiting for a couple of days and they were dropping me off at the airport. I'm in my thirties now, but when I close my eyes and listen to their voices in the front, I easily time-travel like a Kurt Vonnegut character to the days of being shuttled back and forth to soccer practice.

Honestly, it really feels like yesterday. My dad was just yelling at me to wear my shin guards, and here I am now with those adolescent sports-related scars fading away.

"Don't Let the Sun Catch You Crying" is a song Paul McCartney covers on one of his live albums. We were listening to it on the way to the airport, and the title of the song saved me from spiraling into misery.

We're all getting older. There's nothing we can do about it except make the most of our time here.

But obviously, we're running out of time. Please don't give up on your dreams because there's still enough time to get to what you need to get to. However, you can't afford to put it off another day.

Live like a fruit fly.

You Are the One

So why the love affair with the Star Wars trilogy?

Well, it's not just that series. It's the Matrix trilogy as well.

These films are packed with cutting-edge special effects, killer action sequences, and light-years worth of quotable lines. But that has very little to do with my infatuation.

Luke Skywalker is the underdog of all underdogs. He was just some kid with a bad haircut from a small town out in the sticks. He follows his gut and a trail of breadcrumbs, learns the way of the Force, and ends up saving the universe from the most evil of empires.

Thomas Anderson, a.k.a. Neo, mainly keeps to himself because he feels a bit disconnected from everything. He knows intuitively there's something wrong with the world, but he just can't put his finger on what it is. One evening, alone in the dark, he falls asleep in front of his computer after searching for some sort of revelation. The revelation finds him and he's bathed in breadcrumbs. Neo learns he is The One. The one to free humankind from bondage. He chooses to surpass his potential, make the ultimate sacrifice, and save the world.

I, too, have intentionally kept myself on the fringes of the mainstream. I, too, strive to follow my gut when the cards are stacked up against me. I, too, pick up the breadcrumbs, even in the face of all naysayers. I, too, attempt to save the world from the most evil of empires.

But the empire in my crosshairs does not consist of laser-gun wielding stormtroopers or kung-fu capable agents of a robot society.

The nemesis I battle is societal conditioning.

It separates us from the truth.

What truth? Well, that depends on how deep you want to go.

The truth is there's more to life than money. There's more to life than incessant worry. There's more to life than competition. There's more to life than always needing to be right. There's more to life than withholding love because you don't want to appear exposed and vulnerable.

Digging deeper, societal conditioning separates us from this truth as well: There's nothing to fear except fear itself. And we create our own fear. Concordantly, unconditional love is all there is.

Now taking it extremely deep, societal conditioning will have us believe that each one of us is a separate entity standing alone in the universe. But nothing could be further from the truth. We are all connected. God, the universe, me, you, this computer I'm typing on, the air we're all breathing at this exact moment and the spaces in between the air. It's all made of the same stuff. The same soul.

Luke and Neo lived as fruit flies. Their chosen destinies were to be saviors. Mine is to deliver the message of truth. Yours could be the same or maybe your destiny has to do with fixing cars, carving turkeys, raising kids, performing root canals, making movies, painting houses, or simply providing a shoulder for all to cry on.

By the way, "Neo" is an anagram for One. As in, *The One*.

Your name could be Hillary or Harold or Susan or even Shlomo, but whatever letters comprise the spelling, you're also The One.

If not you, then who?

You can chose to live up to and even surpass your potential this very instant. Please make this choice soon. You'll not only feel free and happy, but the entire world is depending on you.

Live like a fruit fly.

"What are you waiting for? You're faster than this. Don't think you are, know you are."

—Morpheus to Neo in *The Matrix*

"Everybody can be great.
Because anyone can serve.
You don't have to have a college degree to serve.
You don't have to make your subject and
your verb agree to serve. You don't have to
know about Plato and Aristotle to serve.
You don't have to know about Einstein's theory
of relativity to serve. . . . You don't have to know the
second theory of thermodynamics in physics to serve.
You only need a heart full of grace.
A soul generated by love."

—Martin Luther King Jr.

Over the Top

I recently sat down for lunch at a local sports bar. This place usually has its twenty HDTVs tuned to the pro and college games of the day. But I made camp there at two-ish in the afternoon in the middle of the week and nothing important was going on in the sports world. Instead, just about every TV in the joint was showing match after match of professional arm wrestling.

Different weight classes were represented, complete with in-depth interviews of male and female competitors. And, by the way, this wasn't a cable access show like *Wayne's World*. It was actually a broadcast by a major network, probably throughout the entire county and quite possibly all over the world.

If this doesn't show you that anything in life is possible, nothing will.

These people actually get paid to arm wrestle. Not only do they get paid, but they're also on TV like Jerry Seinfeld and Emeril Lagasse. Not only are they on TV, but after I finished making fun of it with the bartender, I found myself riveted. And I wasn't the only one in the bar glued to the tube while chomping on french fries.

I'm sure it's possible, but I doubt many of these "athletes" accidentally became professional arm wrestlers. More likely than not, they discovered their talent, climbed through ranks of the amateur circuit, and eventually made the big leagues.

And you just know their parents said, "You want to do *what* with the rest of your life?" That's when normal folks consider quitting. But fruit flies press on when the going gets tough.

Be abnormal.

Some of you are probably saying, "But what really are the chances of becoming a professional arm wrestler?"

Obviously, the chances are slim. But what's just as obvious, a select few do whatever they can do to beat the odds. I saw it on TV with my own eyes. You may have to figure out other ways of putting food on the table for a while, but anything and everything is possible.

Other fair questions: What are the chances of becoming an established artist? How does one figure out how to finance college when there isn't enough money lying around? How do I find someone to love me for who I am?

You do whatever you can do to beat the odds.

And if you fail, pat yourself on the back for trying. Believe me, you'll be in the minority.

If you fail and have honestly done all you can, your destiny lies elsewhere. You'll find it eventually. But hurry up.

Don't give up on your dreams. If you don't make it, it's not going to kill you. But giving up on them most surely will.

Live like a fruit fly.

Over the Top,
Part Two

The bartender and I took a break from the flexing forearms on TV to concentrate on a more imperative topic: women.

He began to tell me a story about this girl he was dating who stopped calling him out of the clear blue. It was a relatively interesting little tale, but to be honest, I couldn't wait for him to get to the punch line so I could tell him about my own battle scars.

I heard and processed every word he said, but I was just waiting for an opportunity to jump in.

In sort of a Mad Libs-ish kind of a way, I caught myself trying to finish his sentences to speed up the process to where it was my turn to blab a bit.

The little angelic fruit fly on my shoulder pleaded with me to ease off and be patient.

I really should know better than to rush someone while they're speaking. If we would only just shut up once in a while and pay attention, we would hear the messages provided to us.

I decided to intently focus on every word he was saying. He could tell that I was really involved and, therefore, he became much more animated.

I sat there alertly, waiting to the bitter end.

What clues were uncovered? What mystery was revealed?

Nothing. Zero. Zip. Total waste of my time. I could have told him twenty better stories in the fifteen minutes he took to tell just one.

The devilish fruit fly lounging on my other shoulder said with a conceited smirk, "See, I told you so."

But the angelic fruit fly is the authentic fruit fly voice from within. It's the voice of truth.

Fruit flies force themselves to be good listeners because:

A. They never want to miss a clue, message, signpost, or speck of breadcrumb.

B. It's just polite.

Let's say we sleep for six hours a night (although it's healthier and far yummier to stay in bed for a few more). According to the calculator in my cell phone, that leaves us with eighteen hours to work with. That's 1,080 minutes.

You can afford to spare fifteen (900 seconds) of them on occasion to possibly uncover a road that might lead you to another road that will lead yet to another road that may turn out to be the road to enlightenment.

Live like a fruit fly.

Time-Saving Tip #2

I have two friends who are vegan. Or maybe it's grammatically correct to say: I have two friends who are vegans. Wait. Maybe it's: I have two vegan friends? Two vegan friends have I? Whatever. I don't have time for this . . .

My two friends who are vegan(s) are servers in a vegan restaurant. Vegans may sound like an alien race from *Star Trek,* but they're actually people who refuse to ingest animal products. No meat, no fish, no eggs, no dairy, no nothin'.

I was at a bar with them one night talking about politics and philosophy.

They guzzled beer and chain-smoked cigarettes while I sipped a diet soda.

One of them read me the riot act about artificial sweeteners. He said 10,000 beagles were recently tortured in a Hitleresque testing facility to attempt to demonstrate the limited health risks of a new product.

I was in the bookstore a few days later and bought a large cup of coffee. Trying not to spill it all over the floor, I shuffled over to that little desk full of coffee condiments. I added a bit of skim milk and then reached for a few packets of artificial sweetener. That's when the 10,000 beagles popped into my head.

Snoopy is a beagle, and I just love that little guy. He's got that manual typewriter and that dry sense of humor and has that little yellow bird that follows him around like Tinkerbell.

And real beagles are so damn cute with those floppy ears and expressive eyes.

After deliberating for a very long minute, I decided to go with old-fashioned sugar. Yes, it has more calories, but at least no one will be able to accuse me of aiding and abetting Snoopy killers.

Because I'm basically a dork, I found myself in the bookstore again the next day. I was about to dump some homegrown sugar in my coffee, but I couldn't help but think of those underpaid and mistreated migrant workers who farm the sugarcane.

How could I protect dogs but overlook the plight of my fellow man? And what about the cows that are pumped with all of those growth hormones?

After a long minute, I took a seat at a table with a copy of the new *Rolling Stone* and a cup of uncorrupted coffee.

What's the moral of this little story?

First of all, black coffee just sucks.

More important though, there simply isn't enough time in one lifetime to enter into every battle. The fronts where we take up arms must be carefully chosen. If we spread ourselves too thin, the causes closest to our hearts will not be properly defended.

God bless my two vegan friends for their passionate protection of bunnies, beagles, monkeys, and red-eyed mice.

Obviously, they support Big Tobacco and seemed to be okay with the legal consumption of probably the most abused drug on the planet, i.e., alcohol, but that's somebody else's war.

I like my coffee fairly sweet and I sympathize with migrant farmers, but I don't have time to enlist in that crusade.

Bringing you the message in this book is the trench I fight from. And for this present moment, we're in it together.

So here's the message: don't spread yourself too thin. Find your cause. You probably already know what it is, but if you're unsure, dig around a bit. I have no doubt you'll discover it or it will discover you. Answers always appear when the correct questions are asked.

But please expedite the search. As you rely on others to fight the good fight, others are relying on you.

Live like a fruit fly.

Wisdom in the Deep End

I'm not going to say that my graying hair traumatizes me, but every time I notice it, it's like walking with a tiny shard of glass stuck in my foot. Not exactly excruciating, but a constant irritant.

I was just a kid and now I'm thirty-seven. A majority of my hair is still holding on tightly to its originally black pigment, but I know it's just a matter of time. Each strand will lose its grip. The first domino has been knocked over. The grays are advancing. Nothing will stop them.

My mom didn't let me get haircuts as often as I would have liked. My hair grows very quickly and I'd have a Dr. J 'fro within two weeks of getting clipped. I felt like I looked goofy. That was my only hair dilemma back in the day.

Now that I'm an "adult," I go the barbershop whenever I freakin' want to. But on the other hand, now that I am an "adult," I'm forced to watch, almost in slow motion, as the mixture of black and gray hairs fall to the floor with every snip.

How could this have happened? Where has all of the time gone? I went to sleep last night worried about not having a date for the prom and I woke up today with two-toned hair.

Women say it looks "distinguished." I'd rather look less distinguished.

Sometimes I don't even care so much how I feel about it, but I worry that it makes my parents feel old. I'm sure they're thinking, *We just took this kid home from the hospital and now look at him, he's graying. Where has all the time gone?*

I was reading a book today at the pool. It's a community pool and two guys in their seventies were wading in the deep end. One was totally gray with thinning hair and the other was almost completely bald with just a few strands of gray remaining. Their wives, both with teased, beauty-parlor gray hair, were actually talking about hair in the shallow end.

The guy who was just thinning on top said to his friend, "You know, when I started to go gray, I didn't even want to look at myself. And you know what my father said?

He said, 'It is what it is. What the hell are you going to do about it?'"

It is what it is. This wisdom can be applied to almost every situation that's out of our control.

Buddhist masters ring a bell from time to time to remind their disciples not to let their thoughts drift.

The next time I look into the mirror and notice the advancing grays with their blitzkrieg tactics, maybe it will feel less like glass in my foot and seem more like a ringing bell. A ringing bell reminding me that it is what it is and life keeps moving on, with or without me.

The truth is, what the hell am I going to do about it?

I'll live like a fruit fly.

The Magic Bullet Theory

The divinely inspired Marc Cohn won the Grammy for Best New Artist in 1992.

I recently read somewhere that Marc Cohn was shot in the head in an attempted carjacking. He was rushed to a hospital where surgeons removed the bullet from his temple. He was then released. He's fine. Like it never happened.

It's safe to say that we can add this to the list of miracles.

But why is he so fortunate when just about everyone you read about is dying of cancer?

The answers, if any exist, are probably too cosmically deep for me or anyone else to piece together.

However, what I can tell you with absolute certainty is this:

We have one shot at this life in our present incarnation. Maybe just one shot altogether. It seems as though miracles as well as catastrophes are hiding behind every corner. We'll probably bump into both along the way, but in either case and before you know it, our time here will come to an end.

So . . . stop worrying so much about the trivial.

Yes. I just called your "problems" trivial. And I'm going to say it again: at least 90% of what's incessantly spinning around in your head is trivial.

Trust me, you'll have plenty of chances to deal with real issues. Just go read the news.

But don't forget about the miracles. They happen every day.

The truth is, your life is a miracle in itself. If you only realized this, you'd experience it more often. Smile and be thankful for this present moment.

Live like a fruit fly.

Karma Is a Bitch

I know I have to write this section, but at first I didn't want to. I was really hoping I'd be able to let this guy off the hook but I can't.

Remember that guy who owns the bar? Yes, the one whose brother was killed in the car accident.

He still comes around where I bartend and he's usually a drink or two away from total unconsciousness. Inebriation at this toxic level is pretty much par for the course for him even before he was dealt the tragic hand.

But maybe he's also the card dealer.

He was recently ruthless to these two girls sitting at my bar. They were on vacation, giggling, minding their own business, and he just ripped into them. Calling them fat. Telling them to go home. So on and so forth.

I know he's been suffering, but that's never an excuse to be malicious—especially to innocent bystanders. Normally, I make it my business to stand up to the face of injustice, but because of the situation, my plan was to delicately ask him to ease off. But these two chicks didn't need me to jump to their defense.

As I was about to say something, they leveled him with a barrage of quick comebacks.

But it was so easy for him to be brutal. It seemed to energize him.

Honestly, I'd need all my fingers and toes to count the amount of times I've heard from reliable sources that this guy has an evil streak. But since he's always acted like a gentleman in front of me

Oh No

Sorry for the abrupt stop on the previous page, but I just killed a fly.

I was sitting here typing and I heard a furious buzz near my ear. It flew past my laptop and circled the printer. I swung at him like a ninja and my open hand furiously met up with his little body. He went tumbling and impacted, I think headfirst, into the wall.

He then lost a bit of altitude but quickly regained control. He eventually made a smooth landing a few feet away from the spot on the wall where he nearly met his maker. I'm sure he needed to take a minute to get his bearings, catch his breath, and assess any damage, so he rested just above the pillow on my bed.

I calmly got up from my chair, picked up one of my flip-flops, and murdered him in cold blood.

On the way to the bathroom to get a piece of toilet paper that I would surely need to exhume his remains from the wall, guilt spread through my body like the poison of a cobra bite.

I know it's just a fly, but the guilt overwhelmed me.

Why did I do it?

My attorney, the sniveling ego, put a defense together in no time. "That fly probably would have had babies in here and then your room would soon look like the elephant's den at the zoo."

I initially concurred with my counsel, but it didn't alleviate the pain. I knew I was only justifying. So why *did* I kill it?

Simply, because I could.

It was in front of me, it was moving slowly, so I didn't hesitate with my act of heartless violence. I easily could have let it buzz on, and I'm sure it wouldn't have affected my path at all.

Dwelling in guilt is a waste of time, but we can learn from regret.

Two lessons here:

One: We cannot take a life just because we can. Just because we think it won't amount to anything. Who are we to know the cosmic consequences? Plus, if we believe that everything is connected, we're actually killing a part of ourselves. And that can't be a good thing if we're trying to gain spiritual and physical ground in this lifetime.

Two: There are proverbial open hands just waiting to swat at us. Like a tornado, it could come at any time without warning. One minute we're anxious about a cryptic e-mail sent from our boss, and the next, well . . . the paramedics are making that dreaded phone call to our unsuspecting families.

I hope that little fly was enjoying his day and not worrying too much about what may or may not happen in the future.

Because obviously, thanks to my murderous ways, his worry would have been in vain.

Live like a fruit fly.

(And glance over your shoulder from time to time.)

Karma Is a Bitch
(continued)

Honestly, I'd need all my fingers and toes to count the amount of times I've heard from reliable sources that this guy has an evil streak. But since he usually acts like a gentleman in front of me, I've discounted the veracity of what I've been told.

After being an eyewitness to the way he treated those two girls, it's possible and even probable his dark side exists. But even still, I was going to afford him the benefit of the doubt.

That benefit dried up a few weeks later when he was back in my bar, verbally abusing a bunch of gay guys who collectively weighed less than he did.

He was obviously disgusted by their sexual orientation and the vodka in his brain was pushing him toward violence.

I sensed that someone's face was about thirty seconds away from contact with a solid fist. At that point, I decided to make sure it was going to be his face before anyone else's.

My hate for bullies eclipsed the sympathy I have for him about losing his brother.

Sometimes we're forced to reach into our dark sides to defend what needs to be defended.

No punches were thrown, and this story ends with the instigator leaving the bar with his tail between his legs.

Of course you're free to believe what you wish about karma. But if I were a betting man, I'd risk all my chips on the following being true: what goes around comes around.

Maybe this guy is holding these horrible cards because he dealt them to himself. Just maybe the compounding years of malice directed at undeserving targets consequently programmed the universe to deliver the car accident.

Or maybe it's totally unrelated. Obviously bad things happen to good people as well.

Events may unfold either out of chaos or by divine connections. But since we can't know for sure, the Golden Rule paves the way. Treat others the way you'd like to be treated. Not only because it's honorable, but also for self-preservation. Because in some form or another, what goes around may just come around.

Live like a fruit fly.

Vegas, Baby!
Vegas!

A close friend of mine since the seventh grade lives on the Upper East Side of Manhattan. He's got a six-figure salary, a posh pad, and an entire network of hip dudes and beautiful women programmed into his cell phone. He's also miserable.

And by miserable, I don't mean he gets upset at stuff once in a while. By miserable, I mean he experiences raw misery almost every day of his life.

His job is killing him.

And by killing him, I don't mean that he has trouble getting out of bed Monday mornings like the rest of us. By killing him, I mean that it's killing him. Literally. As in: it will be the cause of his death.

For now, the stress is manifesting as anxiety attacks. He's in good shape, but is headed for the heart attack highway and he's only thirty-six.

Oh, and by the way, he landed this current job because the woman who previously had it was forced to resign. She had a heart attack.

But it's not just his unfulfilling gig that's causing him to wake up depressed every day.

The city is getting to him. For the most part, the people in his circle are on the borderline of being soulless. They wait in line at the swanky clubs, drink like fish, throw money around, and if they have anything to say for themselves, it's primarily about their Range Rovers and homes out in the Hamptons.

He had a good time running with this crowd for a while; but the little kid inside, the one that I know, isn't having any fun at all. That little kid, the one whose voice is getting louder, just wants to be happy again.

You can't blame him for trying though. Growing up, money was tight in his family so, at first, chasing the big bucks gave him a sense of possible security.

But did climbing the corporate ladder add any real security to his life? No, because he got caught on the corporate treadmill, and six-figures on the Upper East Side means you're living paycheck to paycheck. He's not any more financially, mentally, or spiritually secure than he was years ago.

He called me today with the news that he's moving to Las Vegas. He's got it all worked out and just wants a fresh start. He said it just feels right in his gut. And who can argue with that?

I'm not one who advocates running away from problems because they will inevitably follow you no matter how fast or far you can run.

But he's not running away. He's growing and needs to shed his skin to move on.

We often find ourselves sacrificing our happiness and passions for the prospect of future security and stability. But our lives are happening now. And as we speak, someone is discovering a lump in her armpit. Someone else is just about to crash his car on the way home from work.

Eventually, we must appease that little kid inside of us. Eventually, that little kid will stop putting up with misery and will act out. Today it might be an anxiety attack. Tomorrow a tumor. Eventually, that little kid will have the final say, one way or another.

Security is important. But not at the expense of today.

Live like a fruit fly.

*"Contemplation often makes life miserable.
We should act more, think less, and
stop watching ourselves live."*

—Nicolas de Chamfort

Utah and Omaha

There are times I completely drop the ball with this fruit fly stuff. Last night was one of those times. But thankfully, the evening wasn't a total waste.

I got back home after having dinner out with a friend and although I had plenty of writing to get to, I was just in the mood to lounge around and do nothing.

I found a couple of oranges in the fridge and proceeded to carve them up while checking my e-mail. Within seconds, I was covered in orange carnage. To protect my laptop from the mess I was making, I swiveled around in my chair and turned on the TV with the remote control that was already sticky from the previous night of eating in front of the tube.

Even though the reality show about a tattoo shop was exceedingly more thought provoking than any of the

full-of-agenda cable "news" programs, I kept on clicking until I found footage of Nazi strongholds getting
pummeled by bombs—a subject I never grow tired of.

I eventually washed the orange residue from my hands
and went back to e-mailing. I kept the History channel
on in the background and would peak over my shoulder
every couple of minutes to see if I was missing anything. Just more bombs falling from the bellies of huge
airplanes.

Willpower eventually kicked in and forced me to open
up Microsoft Word so I could get some work done. I
spun around to turn off the WWII documentary because
my remote control only works if it's aimed directly at
the TV.

A still photo of soldiers with mud on their faces illuminated the screen. The voice-over was explaining the
technicalities of the D-day invasion. It's a good thing I
was already sitting because the photo of these kids on
the beach at Normandy just leveled me. Needless to
say, I was sucked in and there was no turning back to
the computer.

156,000 Allied troops, the largest invasion armada in
history, readied themselves. Their mission: save the
world.

Want to talk about fear? These soldiers, barely out of
their teens, crammed into small boats and charged

the beaches. Large caliber machine-gun rounds filled the air. Razor wire and other devilish devices lined the shore. The mortar fire was incessant. The surf was choppy and full of blood. These soldiers, mere children, watched their brothers fall. And all they could do was wait and pray until it was their turn to face the upcoming hell.

On a daily basis we allow our fears to hamper our progress.

I intentionally just used the word allow because everything comes down to choice. We can choose to walk into the bullets and deal with them as they whiz by or we can stay in the boat and take our chances. We may stave off the wounds a bit longer in there, but regret may puncture our hearts nonetheless.

We're afraid to confront our bosses at work, but we know we need to. We're afraid to appear vulnerable in our romantic relationships. We're afraid to roll up our sleeves and face a foe. We're afraid to smile at a stranger.

But our own blood isn't flooding the waters off France. Hopefully, this puts your fears into perspective. And if it doesn't, put this book down now because it just isn't for you.

By nightfall on June 6, 1944, 9,000 Allied soldiers were dead, wounded, or missing. However, on May 7, 1945,

General Eisenhower accepted Germany's unconditional surrender.

You must face your fears. The world is depending on you.

Live like a fruit fly.

*"I have learned over the years that when
one's mind is made up, this diminishes fear;
knowing what must be done
does away with fear."*

—Rosa Parks

Satisfied Mind

Here's everything I know about country music: I don't like it. Actually, I hate it. I've tried and tried to be open to that lone cowboy sound, but my skin crawls with angst just about every time I hear its twang and drawl.

However, because of certain circumstances, I confess I'm a fan, a tremendous fan, of three country/western songs:

"Stand by Your Man" by Tammy Wynette

"Rawhide" by Frankie Laine

"Satisfied Mind" by Jack Rhodes and Red Hayes

"Stand By Your Man" and "Rawhide" were featured in *The Blues Brothers* so I guess I just dig those tunes due to cinematic association. "Rawhide" also does it for me because when I was a kid, my dad often played the *Hell Bent for Leather* record by Frankie Laine. As soon I heard, "Rollin' Rollin' Rollin'—Though the streams are swollen," I'd straddle a yellow broom and gallop around my house like a maniac.

"Satisfied Mind" is an old country standard I wouldn't have known about if Jeff Buckley hadn't covered it.

The song superbly states that having money can't ever and will never substitute for a satisfied mind, old friends, or lost loves.

We spend so much of our lives chasing after, worrying about, and hording the all mighty dollar. Of course we need to eat, purchase Jeff Buckley albums, and put our kids through college, but oftentimes we're blinded by our incessant pursuit of more, more, and more.

Sometimes I get really sad when I look at elderly people. I wonder if they're thinking, *I worked my whole life, breaking my back so I could afford this and that, and now here I am . . . old and frail with only a few years left.* I hope they remembered to smile along the way.

My entire twenties, a third of my life, were wasted because I was basically obsessed with figuring out how to make a buck. Well, of course, they weren't entirely wasted because those years brought me to this perfect moment, but it would have helped if I were aware of fruit flies back then.

Live like a fruit fly.

"Life moves pretty fast.
If you don't stop and look around
once in a while, you
could miss it."

—Ferris Bueller in *Ferris Bueller's Day Off*

I Say It's My Birthday

"NO WISE MAN EVER WISHED TO BE YOUNGER."

—*Jonathan Swift*

According to Swift, I'm not that wise. As I write this, I'm about to turn thirty-eight years old.

I know those of you who are forty-eight or fifty-eight or sixty-eight are probably rolling your eyes and smirking, but if you're twenty-eight, I know that *thirty-eight* sounds over the hill. I was just that twenty-eight-year-old guy myself . . . soon to be forty-eight . . . fifty-eight . . . sixty-eight and so on.

If I force myself to look back with a fine-tooth comb, I can separate all the years and even some of the specific months and days. But viewing it with a wide-angle lens, all I see is an image of one big clump of time that has zoomed by almost undetectably.

I can sit here and bellyache about it, but it's not going to get me anywhere.

When it comes to growing older, my dad says it best, "It's better than the alternative."

Live like a fruit fly.

"Never forget that you must die;
that death will come sooner than you expect . . .
God has written the letters of death upon your hands.
In the inside of your hands you will see the
letters M. M. It means 'Momento Mori'—
remember you must die."

—J. Furniss, *Tracts for Spiritual Reading*

Pondering Paul Simon's "Have a Good Time"

Yesterday was my birthday.

How do I feel about it?

Sometimes I'm down, but most of the time I'm not. My life is in good shape, but sometimes it sure as hell feels like a mess. Am I having a good time? Most of the time, yes. And when I'm not, I really make an effort to have a good time. Otherwise, what's the point of all of this?

Live like a fruit fly.

For Whom the
Bell Tolls

Two days after I wrote about my graying hair on page 105, I crossed paths with a friend who I haven't seen in a while. He eyeballed my head and said, "Damn, Gabe, you're graying."

I sincerely hoped he wasn't talking to me. I looked behind me. There was no one there.

No matter how I sliced it, his words were intended for me. And, in fact, you'd need to be blind not to notice my gray hairs.

However, as Sir Mix-Alot once said, "I like big butts . . ."

So here's my big but . . .

BUT, as his dreaded words threatened to corrupt my mood, my essay of two days earlier popped into my brain.

I would not be a hypocrite. It was time to heed my own advice.

And I quote, "Buddhist masters ring a bell from time to time to remind their disciples not to let their thoughts drift."

My friend was simply ringing the bell, reminding me that it is what it is and life keeps moving on with or without me.

I'm not going to say that I was free and clear of the gray hair blues after that, but I walked away from the encounter with a wise and knowing smile on my face.

Live like a fruit fly.

The Bell Tolls for Me

I met a new girl.

And by *girl* I mean *woman*.

And by *met* I mean "completely fallen for."

A few hours into our first date, I caught her glancing at the side of my scalp.

Dread dread dread dread dread dread dread dread dread.

And more dread.

"Yes, I know. I've got gray hairs."

I really didn't want to say it, but it just flowed out of my mouth like lava.

"I noticed them earlier. I love them."

I think she also said something about it being sexy.

Relief relief relief relief relief relief relief relief relief.

And more relief.

Every situation has a silver lining. Sometimes quite literally.

Live like a fruit fly.

Father (Thinks He) Knows Best

MANY YEARS AGO

IN A GALAXY FAR, FAR AWAY

BEFORE THIS BOOK EXISTED . . .

As soon as we walked through the doors of the bookstore, my dad and I went our separate ways to pursue our own interests. Later, when I went in search of him, I found him in a cushy chair flipping through boating magazines. I sat down in the chair next to him with a book I'd picked up off the shelf and a $4.50 premium coffee beverage.

As I was relishing the lingering butt-heat of the chair's prior occupant and opened the book, my dad turned to me to ask what I was reading. While I don't remember the title, I'm sure it was some book dealing with the universe or God or Eastern philosophy or the Buddha or Kabbalah or Woody Allen.

My dad generally keeps an open mind about my spiritual ways, but that day he knew better.

"Why don't you check out a few magazines on writing?" he suggested.

I just shrugged my shoulders and opened the book to a random page in the middle.

"Give that a rest," he insisted. "You should see all the magazines they have here for writers."

"Those magazines suck," I told him. "They tell you how to win contests and stuff. They're for people who'd do anything to see their name in print."

"Just do me a favor and go look."

Jewish guilt. I'm usually impervious, but my dad can wield it like the dark side of the force when he wants to.

"Fine," I said, and I let out an exaggerated sigh as I got up from the comforts of the chair.

Two minutes later, I brought back a stack of so-called writing magazines. Instead of thumbing through them in chunks like I wanted to, I went page by page to see if any of the articles piqued my interest (but mostly to appease my dad). They didn't.

After going through a couple of the magazines, I came across an article titled something like, WHAT TOP AGENTS ARE LOOKING FOR IN A NEW CLIENT.

This agent's wish list went something like this:

"I'm looking for someone who's energetic and won't be shy with press coverage." I identified with that.

"I'm looking for someone with a writing style that just captures people." I identified with that, too. *"Most important, I'm looking for someone with a book that can change the world."*

That stumped me. My brain scrambled for a planetary panacea, but I came up empty. I dropped the magazines to the floor and took a sip of my room-temperature coffee beverage. As the liquid made its way down my esophagus, the words "live like a fruit fly" flooded my consciousness. Thinking back now, I could swear I also heard the *ta-da* of trumpets.

This fruit fly invasion of my consciousness had come to me once before, probably four years earlier. It had popped into my head while I performed a mundane task required by the dismal corporate sales jobs I was suffering through. At the time, I had no idea what to do with the concept, so I just let it float away with all of the other mental trash of the hour.

But sitting there in the bookstore with my dad, I'd already had a quarter of the book written in my head before I had a chance to borrow a pen from one of the cashiers. And now here we are at the end of page 139.

As much as we may want to discount the advice of those closest to us, we must remember to remain open to the constant flow of breadcrumbs. Because sometimes, actually oftentimes, father really *does* know best.

Live like a fruit fly.

Word to Your Mother . . .

I was watching *Queer Eye for the Straight Guy* one night and in this particular episode, the Fab Five was . . . Okay, stop laughing. I'm serious. It's really not that funny. Yeah, whatever . . . like you didn't tune in from time to time.

Anyway, as I was saying before you rudely interrupted, in this particular episode, the Fab Five was helping out a guy named Hector. Being a typical, macho, straight guy, Hector probably couldn't tell the difference between Taleggio cheese and toe cheese. But as the program progressed, he was schooled in the fine arts of skin care, fashion, and *fromage*.

Thom, who has an annoyingly unnecessary silent "h" in his name, was the interior design specialist on the show and his skills were put to the test. Hector's house needed to be appropriately outfitted because he returned home in a wheelchair after serving his country in Iraq.

Jumping ahead to the last segment: The house looked great, a huge party is prepared for, and yadda yadda yadda . . . unbeknownst to Hector, the doctor who performed the miracle operation that saved his life was invited to the party. When he showed up, Hector's mom gave him a big fat hug and through tears said, "Thanks for saving my baby."

Hector was a brave soldier and will always be a tough, independent New Yorker. Regardless, he's still and will eternally be his parent's child.

Throughout the episode, it was clear that Hector was annoyed at the constant mothering, but it was also obvious that he let his mom and dad off the hook because he totally appreciated their help.

Don't get me wrong, when I visit my parents, and my dad tells me to check in from time to time if I stay out late, I feel like screaming. Sometimes I do.

And trust me, when my grandma, my dad's mom, tries to put her foot down with my dad, he feels like going berserk. And sometimes he does.

I'm sure most of you have been in similar situations.

Regardless of our age, net worth, titles, or accomplishments, we need to let our parents off the hook when they treat us like scatterbrained little children. Not only is it the right thing to do because they're usually only looking out for our well-being, but more important, we cannot allow ourselves to forget about Einstein's Theory of Relativity.

What exactly does this theory state? I'm not too sure to be honest. I think it has something to do with time and the perception of moving objects through space.

Let's just pretend it's applicable to what I'm about to say: From our perspective, we've grown up so quickly. The years whizzed by as we made the journey from grade school to gray hair. But from our parents' perspective . . . well, we might as well be hatchling fruit flies. It doesn't seem like it took a long time to get to where we are, but to Mom and Pop, it all happened in an almost imperceptible flash.

Hector's mom wasn't trying to be cute when she thanked the doctor for saving her baby. Hector is her baby.

Live like a fruit fly.

"I never think of the future. It comes soon enough."
—Albert Einstein

Queer Eye,
Part Two

There's actually a reason why I caught that episode of *Queer Eye for the Straight Guy*.

The final hour of *The West Wing* reruns ended at 2:00 AM and the boys from *Queer Eye* took over on the Bravo network from there. I scrambled to turn off the tube when I heard the nerve-grating theme song, not because I didn't like the show but because my ex-live-in girlfriend was a huge fan of the show and I'd always tease her about it. That theme song could send me traveling back in time to the year we spent as a dynamic duo, and it would make me sad.

But before I could turn the TV off, I was sucked into this particular episode because it was billed as *Queer Eye's* "most deserving straight guy." And once I saw Hector in the wheelchair, heard his story, and felt his undying positive vibe, I was sold.

Since I'm a big softy and a hopeless, or better yet, hopeful romantic, I just loved the fact that his fiancé didn't leave him after his crippling war-related accident.

After a commercial break, she was talking to the camera and said something like, "I love him so much and would do anything for him."

And then she started to cry. And then I started to cry.

And then it hit me like a ton of Taleggio cheese.

If you're thinking about marrying someone who doesn't love you unconditionally—unconditionally meaning to such an extent that he or she can be moved to tears by just being candid about it—give it a little time and then get out. If you're thinking about marrying someone who doesn't fully support you, give it little time and then get out. If you're thinking about marrying someone who you don't blindly trust with your life, give it a little time and then get out.

As De Niro's character says in *Casino*, "When you love someone, you've gotta trust them. There's no other way. You've got to give them the key to everything that's yours. Otherwise, what's the point?"

A fruit fly has a lot to do and not a lot of time to do it in. It would rather buzz around alone than waste time with the wrong fruit fly.

You're everything that's good in this universe and you deserve it all.

Live like a fruit fly.

(FYI, Hector isn't paralyzed and one day will walk again.)

Parenthood

Ten years before Keanu Reeves became our savior in *The Matrix*, he suited up as the grungy Tod Hawkes in the movie *Parenthood*.

Steve Martin was brilliant in the flick; but, as far as I'm concerned, the most poignant line was written for Keanu's character:

"You know, Mrs. Buckman, you need a license to buy a dog, to drive a car—hell, you even need a license to catch a fish. But they'll let any butt-reaming asshole be a father."

Please don't be selfish. Please don't have kids just because you think they'll be fun to play with and dress up. Please don't have kids because it justifies the big house you bought or legitimizes your status as an adult. Please don't have kids just because "that's what you're supposed to do" after you get married.

As I'm sure you can remember, even under the most *Brady Bunch*–like conditions, growing up isn't easy. And as I'm sure you know, making it as a grown-up isn't a walk in the park either.

Turn on the news tonight. Not the dumb local news but the national broadcast and see how scary things have become since we were in diapers. Every previous generation could say the same, but now with terrorism and the threats to our dear Constitution from the inside, God only knows when the pendulum will swing back to the innate feeling of safety we once took for granted.

But if you're emotionally, financially, physically, and spiritually prepared to have children, I wish you the best. As long as your intentions are pure, I have faith things will work out as right as rain.

However, I must remind you that your time here is extremely limited.

If you've lived enough for yourself and have reached a point where you're entirely ready and completely committed to think of your children first in every instance for the next twenty years or so, we can surely use a new batch of fruit flies that are raised to spread love and make the world a better place for us all.

Live like a fruit fly.

Twin Towers

"I DIDN'T CARE ANYMORE WHAT PEOPLE WERE SAYING.
I JUST NEEDED TO FOLLOW MY GUT."

—*Hillary Friedland*

Hillary, my sister, has twin boys and they're just about the yummiest little kids of all time.

One twin quickly unfolded into a chatterbox. The other didn't say much in the beginning, and my sister was convinced he had a hearing deficiency.

Wait, wait, wait.

How can *my* little sister have kids?! This is just too crazy . . . she was just ten, which means I was just fourteen, and I was spitting on the carpet in her room to piss her off. And now she's a mom? (A damn good mom.)

But as I was saying: . . . and my sister was convinced he had a hearing deficiency.

Wait.

That's my sister's quote up there at the top of this essay, and I initially typed "Hillary Berman." My brain refuses to remember she's not a Berman anymore. I still can't get over that my kid sister is married, let alone the mom to twin boys! Okay, let's move on now.

Anyway . . . and my sister was concerned he had a hearing deficiency. Since my mom is a speech and language pathologist, she tried to convince my sister that my nephew's hearing was fine. My mom's speech buddies even concurred. Although my sister was temporarily pacified, she eventually made an appointment with a pediatric ENT doctor because she "just needed to follow her gut."

It turns out that you could have sailed a ship in the sea of fluid found in my nephew's ears. He was fitted with surgical tubes, his hearing is perfect, and now he's quite verbose.

Who knows how this one little problem could have snowballed if my sister didn't follow her gut. Maybe his hearing would have been permanently damaged . . . maybe it would have led him to have early developmental problems . . . maybe it would have led him to being held back in school . . . maybe it would have led him to hanging around with the wrong crowd . . . maybe it would have led him to getting involved in drugs . . . maybe it would have led him to join the mafia . . . and maybe he would have had to off his uncle Gabe. So, it wasn't only my nephew's hearing that depended on my sister following her gut, but my life depended on it, too!

We all know that the "follow your gut" wisdom isn't only applicable to new moms.

No matter who you are and no matter the weight of a situation, do not waver from your gut's directives. The implications, as I'm sure you've realized in the past, could be disastrous.

For those of you who have followed your gut and it hasn't delivered you to where you thought you wanted to be, have patience. You are where you need to be.

Our gut is our inborn GPS connected to the source of all sources. Follow it blindly. Trust it implicitly.

Live like a fruit fly.

Twin Towers with a Twist

I called the previous section "Twin Towers" because in it I talk about my sister's twins. But after giving it a thorough once-over, something else revealed itself.

My sister's job sometimes required her to be in the Twin Towers, but because she'd gotten married on September 1, 2001, and went on a two-week honeymoon, she was thankfully not in New York City on September 11.

I think it's time for me to stop forgetting that my sister is married just because I have a hard time thinking of her as a grown-up.

Thankfully, life keeps on going.

But life is fragile. Don't waste a nanosecond of it.

Live like a fruit fly.

The Dreaded Phone Call

I wouldn't trade my parents for anything. I'm blessed to have them both alive and healthy. And you know what, I think they lucked out with me, too. I was a pretty good kid.

Of course I did some dumb stuff like breaking things around the house, and I'm sure my procrastination on school projects was annoying as all hell; but, for the most part, I think my parents really lucked out.

Because my parents rarely got mad at me, when they did, the injustice of their anger felt monumental. How could they be so furious for something so inconsequential? With me of all people? Didn't they know that everyone else was skipping school . . . and smoking cigarettes . . . and sneaking sips of beer?

Jump ahead fifteen years:

As I admitted earlier, I've had more than a dozen unsuccessful jobs. Whenever I told my parents I'd either been fired or quit, they would react like I'd been arrested for vehicular homicide.

"Oh, Gabe, how could you?"

The disappointment and disgust was unbearable. So unbearable that I'd wish to be stricken with some rare disease or nightmarish ailment just to show them how minor my employment hiccups were in the grand scheme of things.

(Thank God not all prayers are answered.)

The point of this is: Yes, kids are big pains in the asses and need to be disciplined at times. And yes, you want your kid to be successful when he or she grows up. But please be mindful of the big picture. Don't hold grudges. Don't withhold your love out of anger. Life is too short.

Unfortunately, the dreaded phone call in the middle of the night will remind you of that in a hurry.

My dad's best friend got the call early in the morning. His son, who was my age, crashed his car into a tree on the way to school. He died in his older brother's arms.

It could happen to any of us. It will happen to some of us. Guaranteed. And if my dad's friend could have his son back, I bet he wouldn't mind if he grew up into that guy who shovels elephant crap at the circus.

Love like a fruit fly.

*"If you bungle raising your children,
I don't think whatever else you do
well matters very much."*

—Jacqueline Kennedy Onassis

Speedy Delivery

I'm quite psyched to report that I'm officially dating the girl from page 134. Rather than use her real name, I'm just going to call her . . . um . . .

The Girl I Am Dating.

The Girl I Am Dating and I were recently having lunch at a beachside café. She got up to go to the bathroom, so I was left alone with my sandwich and giddy thoughts about how fortunate I was to be with such an extraordinary woman.

"Excuse me."

Pause.

"Excuse me."

Some guy in his early forties at the next table was try-ing to get my attention. He looked *Miami Vice* slick. So did the two younger women sitting on either side of him.

"Do you live here?" he asked.

"Yep. Why?" I asked, but in a "who wants to know?" kind of a way. It's the remnants of the New Yorker in me.

"Is your name Gabe? Gabe Berman?"

Queue up the *Twilight Zone* music.

I was a millisecond away from asking how he knew me, before I realized he recognized me from my mug shot in my column. It happens from time to time.

He confirmed it for me by saying, "I *knew* that was you. I read your column every week."

I smiled a full, genuine smile.

"Yeah man, I never miss it because I love seeing what you have to say."

I was totally gushing. Not embarrassed; but just com-pletely elated.

The Girl I Am Dating made it back from the bathroom, and the guy explained to her that he recognized me. He and I exchanged e-mail addresses and then went back to our meals.

Sitting back at our table, I took off my sunglasses, put my right hand on The Girl I Am Dating's left knee and calmly said, "Do you see how perfectly connected the universe is?"

She lovingly covered my hand with her own and nodded affirmatively.

I'm not relaying this story so I can show you how cool I am (but it is pretty cool isn't it?). There's actually a point to be made here (besides how cool I am).

About an hour earlier, while I was driving my car to pick up The Girl I Am Dating, the new manager of the bar I work for had called to cut me from the bartending schedule on Sunday nights.

At the time, anger flooded my consciousness, which was immediately followed by feelings of betrayal. Then fear. How was I going to get by with less money? How was I going to make it? I was doomed for sure.

I put the pedal to the metal and drove without being present because I was pissed off and nervous. But then, out of nowhere, kind of like that falling feather in *Forrest Gump*, an invisible but very evolved little fruit fly landed on my shoulder.

It whispered in my ear, "Look for the silver lining."

I took my foot off the accelerator and let the car slow down a bit before I continued to give it gas again.

A silver lining. I knew I'd find one if I forced myself to look for it.

Silver lining: The call from the new manager was actually a wakeup call, a wakeup call from my destiny. The voice on the phone said, "We're taking you off the schedule on Sundays." But it was code for, "You don't need this. Trust your writing. Rely on it. Get focused and make it happen."

In other words: Use the Force, Luke. Let go.

Besides sitting there with my grilled chicken sandwich and the glow of a budding new relationship, when The Girl I Am Dating got up for the bathroom, I honestly was also thinking, *Am I talented enough? Can I really make it just with my writing? I wish there was some way to know.*

And I kid you not, that's when I heard:

"Excuse me."

Pause.

"Excuse me."

Obviously I can't explain the metaphysics behind it, but it seems as though answers and breadcrumbs find you faster when you remember to remain aware. With everything you've got, search for the silver lining. You'll find it. And then your destiny will find you.

After I paid the check and overtipped the waiter, the guy who recognized me said, "Hey, Gabe."

I looked up and he continued, "It really was such an honor to meet you."

I replied, "Thank you. But trust me; it was such an honor to meet you as well."

Live like a fruit fly.

"To be nobody but yourself in a world which is doing its best, night and day to make you like everybody else means to fight the hardest battle which any human being can fight and never stop fighting."

—E. E. Cummings

I Love You, Too

Phew . . . <wiping sweat from brow>

I just finished cleaning up my desk. It's a task I force myself to confront every couple of months.

I found an old birthday card under a stack of junk mail. It's an unassuming little card that says:

> "FOLLOW YOUR DREAMS, TRANSFORM YOUR LIFE."
> —*Paulo Coelho*

A fruit fly mantra for sure.

This quote probably deserves its very own page, but for now, I want to turn the spotlight toward the sender of the card.

We don't talk or see each other as much as we should, but she's been one of my closest friends since the first week of college. I've had a crush on her since then as well, but that's a story for another time.

Minutes before Ground Zero earned its name, she actually felt the thunderous vibrations produced when both airplanes pierced the towers. She was in an adjacent building and soon became one of those people we all saw on TV. Dust-covered, panicked, and fleeing on foot as the colossal skyscrapers collapsed behind them.

I knew my parents were safe on Long Island and my sister was on her honeymoon.

After mentally accounting for my immediate family, I couldn't focus long enough to think of anyone I'd want to get a hold of. My hometown and my country were under attack and my thoughts were running wild.

I scrolled through the address book in my cell phone and there she was. When I saw her name, my jaw tightened in terror.

As I'm sure you remember, 9/11 wasn't an easy day to get through to anyone in New York. First call to her: busy single. Second: busy single.

I knew my experience was inconsequential compared to everyone who was actually in the trenches of the situation. Regardless, fear and rage was getting the best of me.

I took a deep breath.

Third call: She answered. I heard her say, "Hello?" The sound of her voice made me cry. (Teary now as I'm writing this.)

I asked her if she was all right and she said yes, but she needed to go because she was scrambling to get in touch with her grandma. My instinct was to tell her just one more thing, but I had to pause for a second before I did.

Her name, followed by the words, "I love you," found its way out of my mouth. She said it back and then hung up.

For some reason, it wasn't easy to say. It was so utterly revealing. I felt naked saying it. Even in that moment I was worried about how she was going to receive those three words. But I knew I had to say it so I did.

Since then, I say it whenever my gut tells me to. I randomly announce it more often to my parents and to my sister. If I feel it for the girl I happen to be seeing at the time, I have no other choice but to look her in the eye and declare it. If she's not ready to hear it, well, too bad. That's life in the big city of the adult world.

And my friends, life is too short to stand on ceremony. I don't ever want to regret not saying it if, god forbid, I never have a chance again. And you won't want to live with that regret either.

Now say it to yourself, give yourself a big hug, and let's move on.

Live like a fruit fly.

"*At the touch of love, everyone becomes a poet.*"

—Plato

Summer Camp

I always do myself a favor by not listening to naysayers.

Metaphysically speaking, pessimism is just an extension of our ego. It provides us with an obstacle to overcome.

Forgetting about the mysterious spiritual world for a moment, the naysayers are usually dead wrong anyway. Nine times out of ten, they're only projecting their own fears onto the situation.

Take my buddy Rob, for example. I mentioned him back on page 16 and later on page 177. He's the one who packed up all of his crap and moved out to Vegas like he said he would.

The naysayers, and there were plenty of them, said stuff like, "You're going to miss New York. What are you going to do in Vegas anyway? Trust me, Rob, you're making a big mistake by leaving and blah blah-blah blah-blah."

But he knew in his heart that it was time for him to move on. He gave the proverbial stiff arm to the naysayers and so far, he's living happily ever after.

The naysayers favorite thing to do is counsel you on relationships. They think they have all the answers.

"Don't move to fast!" they warn.

"Don't show all of your cards!" they squawk.

But trust me, they wish they had the guts to lay it all on the line.

And seriously, what kind of advice is *don't move too fast?* I've got news for you; we can't afford to move slowly. Like I've said before, just go and turn on MSNBC for five minutes. Entire cities are being wiped out by natural disasters, bloody wars are being fought over nothing, women who live down the block from you are getting raped, kids are kidnapped on a daily basis, etc., etc.

Do you think we have the privilege of leisurely strolling through life? Do you think moving slowly is an option? My friends, we only have this present moment. Make the most of it.

My sister just told me this story the other day: One of her husband's best friends died a couple of years ago. He went to bed and never woke up. The autopsy showed he had a heart condition. He was my age.

At the funeral, his girlfriend turned to my sister and said, "I never even got a chance to let him know that I love him."

I can't say for sure, but I bet she was trying not to move too fast.

Counselors and kids in summer camp don't act this way. As we all know from our youth, the bliss of summer is very short-lived. The dreadful school year finally ends and then the next thing you know, the stores are advertising back-to-school sales. So, in camp, when two kids meet, they're forced to go from zero to sixty in two seconds. Hands are held and love isn't held back because they know they'll be back in another disgusting math class soon enough.

Give the stiff-arm to the naysayers. Follow your heart with relationships. Play it as cool as you want, but don't waste too much time. The right person for you will appreciate your summer-camp mentality.

And if the love fades or things go awry, pay no attention to the naysayers and their "I-told-you-so" attitudes. At least you had the moxie to follow your own path. Because that makes all difference.

Live like a fruit fly.

Break On Through

Here's a story of triumph.

There once was a young man who was out to dinner with his aunt, uncle, and cousin. It was the first night of Rosh Hashanah, the Jewish New Year, and families were celebrating with festive meals.

While this young man was pouring a bit of the house dressing on his salad, a young woman entered the restaurant. She was beautiful. Stunning. Breathtaking. A work of art.

The young man thought she was simply perfect. He said to himself, *God's a real showoff sometimes.*

She sat at a table with a decently large group of people and the young man returned his attention back to the small plate of lettuce, cherry tomatoes, and cucumber slices.

His cousin engaged him in conversation, but the young man's focus turned inward and he floated back in time.

The young man actually knew the young woman. Well, he knew of her. He used to see her out in a local pub. She'd stand away from the crowd, sipping wine with a friend. The young man was just one of many who were in absolute awe of her.

So he time-traveled, like that Kurt Vonnegut character, two or three years back to the last occasion he saw her. He thought, just as he always had, *What guy gets to kiss this girl?*

His cousin's voice ripped him out of his self-imposed, mental wormhole and the young man found himself in the middle of a discussion about professional basketball. Out of his mouth came, "Jordan of course is phenomenal. I mean, he's sick. But if I had one pick, I'd still take Magic in his prime."

The young man looked across the restaurant to see what his old crush was up to.

Believe it or not, he caught her staring at him. They both rushed to divert their eyes.

His cousin's voice became muted. The waiter placed a healthy portion of breadcrumb-covered salmon in front of his nose, but his appetite had left the building.

He slowly lifted his head again to look in her direction. Once again, their eyes met. This time she didn't scramble to look away. Neither did he.

The young man's uncle asked him how his food was. He picked up his fork, sampled the fish, and smiled for his uncle.

There's a scene in the movie *About Last Night* when Rob Lowe repeatedly caught Demi Moore staring at him in a nightclub. Toward the end of the evening, Lowe walked up to her and said hi.

She basically retorted, "What the hell do *you* want."

He said something along the line of, "Weren't you looking at me?"

To which she said, "There's a clock above your head."

So the young man looked behind him to see if there was a clock above his head, but the walls were bare.

The uncle appeared to be talking, but the young man interrupted with "I'm sorry to cut you off. But I have to ask you something. How inappropriate is it to ask out a girl, on Rosh Hashanah, in front of her whole family?"

The young man's uncle thought about it for a moment and answered, "Very inappropriate. I wouldn't do it. But, if you have the guts . . ."

Here's the interesting part of this story: The young man, just months before, set his life on a spiritual course. He read every enlightening book he could get his hands on. Within a short time, he was convinced that fear didn't exist and that love was all there is. But in this moment, sitting there with his family and piece of salmon, fear was cornering him like a pack of wild dogs.

Fear of what? Fear of knowing what he had to do. Fear of knowing that he couldn't back out. Fear of knowing it was time to practice what he preached (to himself).

Eventually, the uncle paid the check and the young man was the last to get up from the table.

The young woman was in the middle of eating dinner, but like a torpedo, the young man was headed directly for her. He wished he had nerves of steel, but the truth was, he didn't. He was scared. But as everyone knows, torpedoes do not change course once fired.

Maintaining a proper distance but still standing right over her, the young man said, "Hi. We used to see each other out all of the time."

She smiled and said something but he couldn't hear it. All blood and muscle was focused on trying not to visibly shake.

The young man handed her his business card and said, "If you want to hang out, give me a call."

He walked away.

What did the young man do next? Flowing with confidence, he returned to the young woman's table. But this time, free of fear. And what did he say? Word for word, and making sure to make eye contact with all present, "By the way, that was, by far, the most stressful experience of my life."

They all cracked up. She smiled and put her head down. She was embarrassed but definitely thought it was cute.

How does this story end? The following day, the young woman called. Shortly after that, the young man actually became the guy who gets to kiss this girl. They dated, very seriously, for over a year.

Have you figured out who the young man is?

It's Mitch Cumstein, my old college roommate.

Obviously, or maybe not so obviously, that's just a little nod to *Caddyshack*.

Man, I couldn't believe I was kissing this girl. We'd go to the movies, and I'd pop up right before the flick started to grab some Sno-Caps and Twizzlers. When I got back, there she was, sitting in the seat, looking delicious, waiting for me to sit down so we could resume our handholding.

So what's the moral of the story?

When I handed her my business card, the fear, the pack of wild dogs, scattered. In that moment I didn't care about results anymore. It didn't matter if she called or not. The only thing that mattered to me was that I fought through the fear.

In that moment, I broke on through to the other side. I know it's just another story about a girl, but for me, it was the day I became a man. A man in this world but not of it. A man cutting his own path. A man who gets the girl.

You can read all the spiritual works you want, but if you don't live and breathe it, you might as well sit down for the night with a cup of tea and a Danielle Steel book.

Like Neo in *The Matrix*, I learned that there is a monumental difference between "knowing the path and walking the path."

People rarely get what they truly want. Why? Because they're afraid to follow their gut and show some guts.

But life is too short not to. You owe it to yourself to be like a torpedo.

Live like a fruit fly.

Impermanence

This is one chapter I never thought I'd have to write.

But there's no getting around the truth.

So without further ado:

The Girl I Am Dating will now be known as The Girl I Am No Longer Dating. But that's just a nickname for her nickname. Her full nickname is The Girl I Am No Longer Dating Because She Freaked Out on Me One Night.

I was totally falling in love with this chick, too. Never have I jelled so well with anyone before. Even though we were only together for a month, I thought for sure she was "the one." But as old Billy Shakespeare once said, "There are more things in heaven and earth, Horatio, than are dreamt of in your philosophy."

I got in bed with her and I felt a disturbance in the Force. And then, out of left field, she hit me with her grievances. To make a short story shorter, she just wanted me to be someone I'm not.

I laid there in her bed, literally shaking for a minute or two.

Fortunately, I was saved by my own fruit flies. The downward spiral came to a halt. My thoughts slowed down. I actually smiled.

I smiled because I knew my intentions were pure with her from day one. I couldn't have handled it all any better. I was as loving and as fun as I could have been. Because of this, I knew the universe was unfolding as it must, and things would work out best for all parties involved.

To give her a quick chance to wake up from the slumber of her misguided priorities, I attempted to show her the other side of the coin. But it was useless. She was convinced. Her mind was made up.

Rich, one of my dearest friends on the planet, had his heart ripped out by a girl a few years back. He really liked her, and I remember trying to get him to say whatever he could to salvage the relationship. But he said, "I never want to convince someone to love me."

Those words resurfaced in my brain as I contemplated my next move. I didn't want to convince her to love me. She should have just felt it.

I felt like Jesus as I got out of bed. Not crucified, but glowing and connected to everything. I calmly stepped into my jeans, sat on the edge of her bed as I tied my shoes, and then made my way back to where she was wrapped in sheets and blankets like a mummy.

I kissed her forehead and closed my eyes. My lips stayed pressed against her skin for another second because I knew it was our last kiss.

She asked me where I was going, and I told her that I had to leave because I knew she'd never love me for me.

I turned around and walked into the sunset.

I lived with a girl once. We lived together for a year and when she broke up with me, I was undeniably devastated. Soon after, Rich sent me an e-mail that simply read, "Don't worry about it man. You're everything that's good in this world."

And so are you.

You shouldn't have to convince anyone to love you. Give them a bit of time to work through their confusions and provide all the info they'll need to choose wisely at the crossroads. But as much as it stings, there are times when you're going to have to calmly put your jeans on and go.

Don't settle for anything less than unconditional love.

Live like a fruit fly.

"I love you, and because I love you,
I would sooner have you hate me for telling
you the truth than adore me
for telling you lies."

—Pietro Aretino

Man's Best Friend

I sent an e-mail to The Girl I Am No Longer Dating. I walked out of her place like a hardened cowboy, but a couple of days later I felt the need to show some humility.

I told her that I missed her. I needed to know if she had a change of heart.

Rob Leone, my wartime consigliore, counseled me against it, but I just had to do it anyway.

He told me she wasn't worth it. He said she didn't deserve me. And he simply didn't want me to give her the satisfaction.

But Rob didn't know the truth. What truth? I didn't care if she thought I was a dork after reading my e-mail. I didn't care if she was sitting there, relishing in her victory. I didn't care if she was filled to the brim with satisfaction.

My only concern was . . . well, let me share this with you first:

I'm a dog lover.

They're loyal and always excited to see you. They catch tennis balls, eat Cheerios off the floor, and bark at strangers.

However, a dog isn't man's best friend. Closure is.

Another fallacy: Time heals all wounds. Total nonsense. Once again, it's closure.

Time only serves as a healing agent with the onset of senility.

If you're anything like me, I'm sure from time to time, you're mentally visited by failed flings like the Ghost of Relationships Past.

But fruit flies don't have time to sit and stew.

She e-mailed me back and like Excalibur stuck in the stone, she wasn't budging.

And you know what, thank god.

I was hoping she had no interest in rekindling. As I said on page 175, you just don't want to convince anyone to love you.

So . . . getting back to where I was before, my only concern was getting this door closed to allow for another to swing open.

And swing open it will. It will for you as well. Humility is the grease that lubricates the hinges.

Live like a fruit fly.

Extra Seconds

We're dying.

Our time here is limited.

Therefore, our time with our loved ones is limited.

And I know you know this. You definitely didn't hear about this death thing for the first time from my little book. But you have to admit, we all live like it's never going to happen.

We sometimes rush our parents off the phone.

We sometimes are too busy to pay attention to the children in our lives.

We sometimes aren't in the mood to pet our dogs.

We sometimes take our significant others for granted.

I've been guilty of all of these and more. However, I will give myself a bit of credit here as well.

Because I try not to let myself forget about the impermanence of all things, I have always given my ex-girlfriend good hugs. I was the hug master.

And I'm not talking about The Girl I Am No Longer Dating. I'm referring to the girl I mentioned back on page 49. The one I'd watch fall asleep. I was so in love with her. We'll call her: The Girl I Was So in Love With.

Not every time, but almost every time we hugged, I held on for just another second before I broke away. In that extra second, I made sure that she felt every ounce of my love for her. In that second, I closed my eyes and gave her everything I had.

There were two reasons for my approach to hugging:

1. It just felt good. For both of us.

2. Just in case. Just in case, for whatever reason, one of the hugs ended up being the last one forever.

The day came and I unknowingly gave The Girl I Was So in Love With my last hug. It's a good thing I took the extra second to make it count because I have absolutely no regrets about it today.

Take the extra second with your loved ones. If you can, spare the time for everyone.

Live like a fruit fly.

Let's Do It for Johnny . . .

I have a huge crush on Diane Lane.

I fell for her back in 1983 when I saw *The Outsiders* for the first time. She played Cherry, the pretty little "privileged" girl who saw through the opaque divisions between the Socs and Greasers. She was eighteen at the time, and I was eleven. I always did have a thing for older chicks.

I recently looked her up online and unlike most humans, she gets more beautiful with every passing year. However, she's still mortal and you can tell she's slightly starting to age.

Why do I take up your precious time with this topic?

1. Maybe she'll read this book and realize we're star-crossed lovers. If so, Diane, sweetie, I'm sorry about the aging comment. It's just a little notice-able around the corners of your eyes. It's no big deal though. I still think you're stunning. So e-mail me or something.

2. Everyone ages and looks eventually fade. It's inevitable.

Oftentimes we chose our life mates based solely on outer appearances.

Of course we want them to be halfway decent people, but as long as they're not ax murderers, we're sold on physical attraction.

Don't get me wrong; I know looks and animal urges are vital. I'm honestly not many notches away from the caveman mentality myself. But I've learned that true love, not lust, keeps a relationship moving forward in a positive direction. Okay, lust, too. But love is what everything needs to be based on.

Because of sorcery and my Jedi-mind tricks, drop-dead gorgeous women have proudly introduced me as their boyfriend. But after one too many mindless squabbles, their true colors eclipsed their outer beauty, and I was no longer able to see the attributes that pulled me in to begin with (yes, Diane, I know some ladies, like yourself, are beautiful to the core).

You can choose a trophy wife or a shallow hunky husband and, for the time being, you'll be a pig in . . . well,
you know. But while you're not paying attention, our
planet is revolving around the sun. Without fail, you'll
wake up one morning next to someone who has aged.
And without fail, you'll become miserable and want to
head for the hills.

There are so many unexpected pitfalls in this brief life of
ours, don't set yourself up for one that can be avoided.

With true love (and some lust), maybe you'll never even
notice the wrinkles.

Live like a fruit fly.

*"Wherever you are, and whatever
you do, be in love."*

—Rumi

Rock the Vote . . . or Not

I know this is coming out of left field, but it's something that needs to be said. Especially in today's day and age:

Vote or don't vote, that's your call. But if you're going to cast a ballot, vote with your heart, not with your pocket-book.

Your entire life on this planet is just a passing blip on the cosmic radar screen.

How would you like your blip to be distinguished from the billions of others? Totally self-serving? Or a blip that voted with its family, its community, its country, and its planet in mind?

Blip like a fruit fly.

Sun Tzu

Back in my corporate days, I'd bring a bagged lunch to work to save some dough. But if I didn't have time in the morning to whip up a sandwich, I'd escape my office around noon and head out to some fast food joint.

On one such occasion, I was trying to enjoy my excessively processed meal while four big guys were harassing a girl with Down's syndrome. I guess she was hired as part of a program and her job seemed to be refilling the napkins and straws, etc. These thugs were really ripping into her, but she tried her best to keep a smile on her face.

The surplus of blood pumping from my enraged heart almost forced me to stand up and take my chances right then and there with hand-to-hand combat. However, the four-to-one ratio—of big guys to me—kept me in my seat.

I decided to remain calm, finish my lunch, and then go to the bathroom to figure things out. After finishing the food I could barely taste due to nerves, I went into the filthy bathroom and stared at myself in the mirror.

I thought of a few clever things to say to the four of them, but I knew they'd just laugh at me and my words. There was no way of getting around it. The pen may be mightier than the sword, but sometimes only the sword is respected and understood.

I thought about my mom and my dad and my sister. I thought about how they would feel if I got really blood-ied up in a fight. I thought about how devastated they'd be if one of these punks pulled a knife and killed me.

But I decided standing up for someone who is unable to stand up for themselves is a cause worth laying your life on the line for.

I loosened my tie. I rolled up my sleeves. I stretched a bit. I made fists so tight that I strained my forearms. Again, I looked into the mirror and saw a game face I almost didn't recognize.

Like in a movie, I shoved open the bathroom door and slowly approached the counter.

I pointed to the one who seemed to be the leader and said, "Hey, you. Come here."

He ignored my request, so I raised my voice and added an angry curse word. This time, he rushed over and only the counter separated us. I told him that he was acting like a disgusting excuse for a person, and he should be embarrassed for how he was treating the girl. He attempted to reply, but I just kept shouting. The three others in his crew came to his side.

My rage and sense of right made me feel powerful. I angrily continued, "God *help* you if you f*#@ with me. You have *no* idea who I am, and I *will* take each one of you down."

I told them they'd be done for if I ever saw them or even heard of them treating the girl badly again. I calmly turned around when I'd said what I needed to say. As much as I wanted to sprint out of there, I made sure to keep a slow stride. I was hoping not to get shot in the back.

I made it out of there unscathed, and I guarantee the four of them will remember what I said and think twice about harassing someone less fortunate than themselves.

There are times we need to unsheathe our swords and go to war. But a carpenter once said, *"For all they that take the sword shall perish with the sword."*

Fruit flies definitely do not want to perish any earlier than need be. Their time here is short enough as it is. However, in extreme cases, fruit flies would rather take their chances in battle than have to live out their lives feeling as though they abandoned a brother or sister.

Walk away from just about every fight. It's almost never worth it. But if your back is literally against the wall or if you need to stand up for someone who cannot stand up for themselves, do what you must.

Live like a fruit fly.

The Fifth Noble Truth

S mile.

Just smile right this second. Give me a nice big smile. C'mon, show some teeth.

Don't argue with me. Just do it. Pretend, just for a second, that you have something to be excessively happy about and smile. Do it as if your life depended on it.

Isn't it amazing that you felt happy in that brief moment of smiling? It's as if your smile fakes you out.

You don't have to be Sherlock Holmes to conclude that in our day-to-day lives, when something makes us feel happy, we smile. But maybe it works the other way as well. Maybe just the smile can make us feel happy. Maybe the smile sends a signal alerting us that things are good and working out well.

Go look at a painting or statue of the Buddha. He's always got that little smile. It's not like he's laughing at a Marx Brothers' movie, but it's obvious by the way the corners of his mouth are slightly raised that he's peacefully content.

Maybe the peace he found made him smile. But maybe the smile made him feel at peace. Maybe it's both.

Maybe we should remember to smile more often. You know, just for the sake of smiling.

Then, if you believe as I believe that EVERYTHING is connected, maybe you'll actually attract the situations that justify your peaceful easy feeling. Maybe the trick to being happy is just using this little "trick."

So here's the plan: smile as often as possible. Especially when you don't feel like it. Of course, your ego is going to tell you that you're being foolish. But fight through that and tell your ego to go to hell by itself. You're only interested in the kingdom of heaven (happiness and peace).

If I'm wrong about this, if the Buddha is wrong, feel free to go back to unconscious frowning.

But you have nothing to lose and everything to gain with a smile.

Live like a fruit fly.

Swing for the Fences

Terrorism.

The Middle East.

North Korea.

Neo-cons.

Natural Disasters.

It's pretty scary out there and, for the most part, it's out of our hands.

Our choices seem to boil down to these two paths: worry or don't worry.

Things are going to unfold the way they must either way.

I'm not delusional. I know the world's problems aren't going to magically disappear if you chose to ignore them (see footnote). But, on the other hand, where is worrying going to get you? Do you think it's going to make anything better? Of course you don't.

So go out there and live your life.

I'll share a little secret with you that may help you sleep better tonight: there's nothing really to worry about anyway. How did I come to this conclusion? All you have to do is look at the past. Good always wins. Evil may percolate from time to time and have its day in the sun, but sooner or later, the good guys prevail.

The bigger they are, the harder they fall. Nazi Germany seemed pretty tough at the time and so did the Soviet Union. And where are they now? In history books.

It seems as though the universe allows evil to dominate from time to time to give the virtuous an opportunity to show virtue. And when the time is right, they'll step up to the plate. So get in the batter's box and wait for your pitch.

Live like a fruit fly.

Footnote: Although rock-solid faith may metaphysically manifest global peace.

Active Forgiveness

I overheard some guy make an anti-Semitic comment to his buddy at my bar the other night. I let it go at first, but he later made the near-fatal mistake of pointing his ignorance in my direction.

I have to be honest with you, in that moment, I completely forgot to remember everything I know about the universe. All of this fruit fly stuff went out the window and I wanted blood. I actually envisioned myself hopping over the bar to get medieval on him.

Thankfully, way back in a corner of my mind, there was a bit of light still shining. It rapidly illuminated the dark tornado of anger circling in my head. By the time this idiot was done spewing, I was already utilizing Active Forgiveness.

Before I explain what Active Forgiveness is, here's what it isn't: It's not about turning the other cheek. It's not about allowing yourself to get hit (with words or fists). It's not about letting a guy get away with spreading hate (I pulled the guy out of the bar and leveled him with logic. He eventually apologized. But as I said on page 116, if he decided to up the ante by raising his hands and therefore putting my back against the wall, vengeance would have been mine).

Active Forgiveness is simply, silently, and sincerely forgiving everybody for everything.

Do you sometimes find yourself thinking about how unfairly your ex handled things? Forgive her or him. Did the waiter screw up your order? Forgive her or him. Did your friend say something inappropriate? Silently forgive. Boss on a power trip? Forgive. Someone in your family do something unforgivable? Forgive.

Forgive, forgive, forgive, and then forgive some more.

Why use Active Forgiveness?

1. You'll physically feel better the moment you earnestly forgive. I'm not sure why, but the stress that churns my stomach completely disappears when I forgive. If today were my last day here, I'm going to do what I can to enjoy it. Feeling less stressed is the place to start.

2. Saint Francis of Assisi said, "It is in pardoning that we are pardoned."

What do we need pardoning from?

From letting others live rent free in our heads.

How often do we replay past events? How often do we dwell on how others have hurt us?

It's all too often. But as we know all too well, our time here is quite limited. We need to keep our heads clear of negative thoughts so we can focus on our passions and be alert to breadcrumbs. We need to keep our heads clear to allow room to be happy. We need to keep our heads clear to remember to love.

3. For those of us on a spiritual path, here's the most monumental reason to master Active Forgiveness. It will make you feel closer to God (or to the universe or however you want to label it). And what's better than that? Nothing.

A few paragraphs ago, I instructed you to forgive the unforgivable. This doesn't mean that you should say to the sister-in-law who completely screwed you, "I know what you did and I still welcome you into my home." Deal with people and their transgressions in any way you see fit. But silently forgive because they are unaware of their actions—in other, more famous words: they know not what they do.

Is this forgiving business easy? It may not be at first. We're surrounded by a society that thrives on harboring ill feelings. But does this seem to be working for anybody?

Society's pressures are strong. It oftentimes feels as if we should follow the herd and hold on to our anger so we don't appear weak. But, please, remember that you have free will. Don't follow the herd. Follow your heart. You're in control of your thoughts and choices. Trust me and trust your gut, it's in your best interest to make the higher choice of forgiveness.

Live like a fruit fly.

"We who lived in concentration camps can remember the men who walked through the huts comforting others, giving away their last piece of bread. They may have been few in number, but they offer sufficient proof that everything can be taken from a man but one thing: the last of the human freedoms—to choose one's attitude in any given set of circumstances, to choose one's own way."

—Viktor E. Frankl, *Man's Search for Meaning*

Why Are We Here?

This question has been asked since the beginning of time, and I'm now going to pass the microphone to the author of *Autobiography of a Yogi*, Paramahansa Yogananda:

"Live each moment completely and the future will take care of itself."

Give that a moment to register.

Live each moment completely and the future will take care of itself.

Until God or science (or both) shows me otherwise, I don't see any purpose other than living each moment completely.

That's it. Thank you very much. Don't forget to tip your cocktail waitresses. Good night.

Live like a fruit fly.

Jim Morrison, Chester Copperpot, and Bobby McFerrin

I n summary:

Pay no mind to what society dictates, live the life you've been born to live.

Always follow your gut.

Don't allow yourself to lose touch with your youth and the child inside.

Appreciate and forgive.

What goes around comes around.

Face your fears and break on through to the other side.

Pursue your passions. No matter what, don't give up. Goonies never say die.

Don't worry, be happy.

Smile.

Love yourself and all others unconditionally.

Have faith. Be faith.

You are The One.

The clock is ticking.

Live like a fruit fly.

Seize the Day

On page 80, I mentioned that my brother-in-law's mom has a malignant brain tumor.

Well, she *had* a brain tumor.

After the funeral service, we all drove over to the cemetery. From the backseat of my parent's car, I read the names carved into headstones.

We've all been to cemeteries, so as you know, I had to walk over a few graves to join up with the rest of my brother-in-law's family. There was something surreal about knowing there were dead bodies under my feet.

It was nineteen degrees that day, but I took a glove off to touch a few of the headstones. While slowly pulling my index finger along the top of one, I took a look around in all directions. Thousands of people who were just like me. They were all little kids once. They all grew up and dealt with this roller coaster of life. They all had dreams about being truly happy. And now they're all gone.

From my perspective that cold day, it's almost like they never even existed.

The Rabbi delivered his consolatory words, and my mind drifted to a scene from my all-time favorite movie *Dead Poets Society*.

Keating, Robin Williams's character, instructs his students to gaze at old class photos in a display case. He asks them to consider if the boys in the faded photos, most of whom have since passed away, chose to live the life they had hoped for. Speaking for those boys from their graves, Keating whispers to his students, "Carpe diem, lads. Seize the day. Make your lives extraordinary."

And from one fruit fly to another, those are the same words I now whisper to you:

Make your life extraordinary. Don't wait until it's too late. Remember this moment because it's the youngest you're ever going to be.

Live like a fruit fly.

Thank You

"IF A MAN DOES NOT KEEP PACE WITH HIS COMPANIONS, PERHAPS IT IS BECAUSE HE HEARS A DIFFERENT DRUMMER. LET HIM STEP TO THE MUSIC WHICH HE HEARS, HOWEVER MEASURED OR FAR AWAY."   —*Henry David Thoreau*

This book *really* couldn't have been written without the people I love (yes, I'm talking to you). A special thanks to Debra Shapiro, who miraculously led me to my brilliant editor Carol Rosenberg at HCI Books. I also want to acknowledge the following musicians to whom I am forever grateful: The Beatles, Pat Metheny, Yes, Sting, Bruce Springsteen, Billy Joel, Radiohead, Paul Simon, Dave Matthews, Bob Dylan, Peter Gabriel, Miles Davis, John Coltrane, Dave Brubeck, Jack Johnson, Ben Harper, Bruce Hornsby, Rage Against the Machine, John Mayer, James Taylor, The Sundays, Coldplay, Sigur Ros, and of course, Jeff Buckley.

About Gabe

Gabe **Berman** is a native
New Yorker who settled in
South Florida after gradu-
ating from the University
of Miami. An epiphany,
a passion, and a trail of
breadcrumbs led him out of Corporate America and
into a writing career. His columns appear regularly in
The Miami Herald and on Alan.com (Alan Colmes
Presents Liberaland).

"Fireflies know nothing of fences or chewing grass or staying put. Fences don't figure for fireflies."

-être the cow

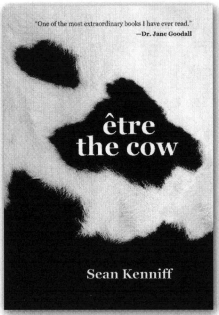

Code 502X • paperback • $11.95

This poignant tale about pushing limits and challenging one's destiny, told through the eyes of a bull at Gorwell Farm, ". . . is one of the most important books written in a generation . . . and it's a story I won't soon forget," says Archbishop Emeritus Desmond Tutu.

6503265R00121

Made in the USA
Lexington, KY
27 June 2017